D1239115

ERRORS IN SEX-ROLE BEHAVIOR IN TEEN-AGE BOYS

ERRORS IN
SEX-ROLE BEHAVIOR
IN TEEN-AGE BOYS

Charles Christopher Harrington

TEACHERS COLLEGE PRESS
Teachers College, Columbia University
New York

ACKNOWLEDGMENTS

As a psychological anthropologist, I am particularly interested in problems of socialization and, in this book, in problems of sex-role socialization in contemporary American culture. This book derives from close contact with John W. M. Whiting; as his student, research assistant, and teaching fellow. My debt to him is immense. I must thank him for the encouragement, support, guidance, and intellectual stimulation which have made this study possible. Thanks are due others at the Laboratory of Human Development at Harvard University, where this study was first conceived: R. Lee Munroe, Ruth Munroe, and Gary Granzberg. Beatrice Whiting has always been a willing and patient listener. Irwin Goffman, Jerome Kagan, David McClelland, Irven DeVore, David Maybury-Lewis, and R. Jay Turner made many essential suggestions.

The study was supported by the Mental Health Research Unit of the New York State Department of Mental Hygiene, which furnished the author financial support, office space, secretarial help, and a research assistant for one summer. Thanks particularly go to that assistant, James Howe, who did half the interviewing, and contributed many valuable insights into these data. Thanks go to John Cumming, Director of the Mental Health Research Unit, and his wife Elaine, who succeeded him during the study. Thanks also go to Dr. Ruth Munroe for her valuable aid in scoring the Franck Drawing Completion Test and to Rhondda Cassetta for scoring the Franck Test, for statistical and editorial help, and for much encouragement; to Gary LaBreche for computer programming assistance; to Sandra Sica and Mary Ellen Matthews for so diligently typing the manuscript through an endless number of drafts; and to Marlene Lesiakowski for her help on the bibliography. Computer time was graciously provided by Syracuse University Computing Center. Giselle Nemeth Harrington, my wife, and Christopher John Harrington, my son, are owed my special and personal gratitude.

Thanks are due to the five agencies who participated in this study, their directors and staff. But most of all, thanks must go to the families and the boys themselves. I must thank them for their hospitality, courtesy, time, and patience. To the boys, who wondered what these "crazy tests" were all about, but nevertheless cooperated, this study is dedicated.

Teachers College, Columbia University
June 1968

CONTENTS

I. INTRODUCTION

Anthropologists, like other social scientists, have devoted much time to discovering the cross-cultural as well as intracultural regularities and consistencies of human existence. Their findings have quickened a burgeoning interest in anthropology. In response to stimulation from psychology and psychiatry, anthropologists have become concerned with the regularities between individuals and cultural institutions, and between individuals at different ages. Thus anthropology has picked up the "dogma" (Kagan and Moss, 1962) that certain behaviors can be related to what happened to an individual before he was, say, ten years old. One of the characteristics of this new field of psychological anthropology, however, is that while it borrows ideas from psychology, it does not accept them without question. If anthropologists are going to use psychological principles to interpret culture, they first make sure that they are valid. In doing so they have generated a fair amount of literature that is of some relevance.

Whiting, Kluckhohn, and Anthony (1958) used the psychological concept of sex identity to interpret a phenomenon frequently studied by anthropologists, male

1

initiation rites. Their cross-cultural study established
the following:

1. A close relationship between mother and son during infancy as a consequence of either (a) their sleeping together
for at least a year to the exclusion of the father, or (b) the
mother being prohibited from sexual intercourse for at least
a year after the birth of her child, or (c) both of these together,
has measurable consequences which are manifested in cultural adjustments at adolescence.
2. These adjustments are either (a) a ceremony of initiation into manhood involving at least one and generally several
of the following factors: painful hazing by the males of the
society, tests of endurance and manliness, seclusion from
women, and genital operations, or (b) a change of residence
which involves separation of the boy from his mother and sisters and may also include some formal means for establishing
male authority such as receiving instructions from and being
required to be respectful to the mother's brother or the members of the men's house.
3. If both the factors specified in (1) are present, the consequences at adolescence tend to be more elaborate and severe
than if only one is present. (1958:368–369)

The authors offered a psychological interpretation of
their findings based upon the concept of sex identity.
This interpretation was further refined and more completely stated by Burton and Whiting (1961), who viewed
the absence of the father as leading to primary cross-
sex (feminine) identity in boys. Initiation rites are designed to overcome primary cross-sex identity and substitute male identity and behavior. If the identity conflict were not resolved, boys would retain behaviors inappropriate to the society's adult male role.

Such use of psychological principles to explain cultural events does not go unchallenged, however. For
example, in 1962 Frank Young proposed a theory of
initiation rites as an alternative to Whiting's. Young
viewed the rites as dramatizations of the male role pre-

paratory to the participation of the initiates in exclusively
male societies. Thus, rather than looking to events in
the life cycle before age ten and relying only upon psychological concepts to explain initiation rites, Young
looked to the patterns of association of adult males in
the whole society. Young might share with Needham a
belief in Durkheim's contention that "whenever a
social phenomenon is directly explained by a psychological phenomenon, we may be sure that . . . [the ex-
planation] is false" (Needham, 1962:126). While Young
formulated his structural explanation as an alternative
to Whiting's, Whiting incorporated Young's position and
argued "that both male solidarity and male initiation
rites are a consequence of conflict in sex identity engendered in infancy" (Whiting, 1962:392).

Before accepting any socio-psychological interpretation, we should examine it and its assumptions closely.
In this case, we will examine the concept of conflict
in sex identity, or "cross-sex identity." Used in refer-
ence to males, this term means that they identify with
women, usually the mother. According to Whiting, the
individual forms "primary" or "optative * sex identity"
in infancy and "secondary" or "subjective sex identity"
in childhood, corresponding to the status arrangements
encountered by him in those respective periods. Primary
cross-sex identity is linked to absence of the father as

---

* Burton and Whiting (1961) distinguish three kinds of identity:
"attributed" (statuses assigned ego by others in his society);
"subjective" (statuses which ego considers himself to oc-
cupy); and "optative" (statuses which ego wishes to oc-
cupy). The aim of socialization is to produce adults whose
three identities are congruent. Optative identity is not always
a conscious wish, and in fact can be assumed to be either an
unconscious wish or a cognitive style; subjective identity,
on the other hand, is conscious. In this report we consider
"optative sex identity" equivalent to "primary sex identity"
and "subjective sex identity" equivalent to "secondary sex
identity." These terms are discussed in the next section.

measured by exclusive mother-child sleeping arrangements and long postpartum sex taboos. Secondary cross-sex identity is formed later and linked to absence of the father as determined by matrilocality. Secondary *male* identity, in contrast, is linked to male influence as measured by patrilocality. The definition of father absence for primary cross-sex identity is different from that for secondary because the domain of the child changes. When the child is an infant, his domain is limited largely to where he sleeps, hence the importance of who sleeps with him. As the child grows, his domain enlarges to include the household, and importance shifts from sleeping arrangements to whether the father is present in the household at all and to the status males possess (for example, in a patrilocal or a matrilocal household).

In the Whiting theory, the relationship of cross-sex identity to behavior, which is of central interest in this report, depends upon the combination of primary and secondary identities. Primary cross-sex identity may be either reacted against or expressed, depending upon the secondary sex identity. Some societies institutionalize a means for resolving an underlying conflict in sex identities (primary, female; secondary, male) in favor of the secondary sex identity. Circumcision-type initiation rites are an example of this. These ceremonies occur in societies which differentiate boys from girls (Harrington, 1968) and presumably teach boys the appropriate male role. Thus they attempt to insure proper masculine role behavior by making it clear that the boys are now men, and are different from the women who have raised them.

If there is conflict between primary and secondary sex identities without a mechanism to resolve it, the individual reaction to primary feminine identity may be an exaggerated masculinity, through which the boy tries to resolve the conflict (see Munroe, Munroe, and Whiting, 1965). Such hypermasculine traits have been linked to feminine identity by several researchers. B. Whiting (1965) explained aggression as "protest masculinity," and found it more often in those societies where the father has low salience in infancy but high status later in life. (See B. Whiting, 1965, for a good summary of the literature on protest masculinity.) Whiting, Kluckhohn, and Anthony consider juvenile delinquency in the United States to be a reaction to underlying femininity:

It has long been known that there is an association between certain types of juvenile delinquency and broken homes. We would predict that the probability of a boy becoming de-linquent in such instances would be highest where the separa-tion of the mother and father occurred during the early infancy of the boy and where she [later] . . . remarried. (1958:370)

Another example would be the *macho* complex among Mexican males (see Lewis, 1951). Reactions of exagger-ated masculinity typically come about when there is an overlaying of male influence upon a child with primary cross-sex identity, as for example may be the case in Cayman (see Howe, 1966). Cultural mechanisms to re-solve the conflict, such as circumcision-type initiation rites, are said to make such individual protests super-fluous.

Cross-sex identity may be openly expressed if the primary and secondary identifications are both feminine. One institutionalized expression is couvade, a set of practices in which the man shares symptoms of preg-nancy and childbirth with his wife (see Munroe, Mun-roe, and Whiting, 1965). Burton and Whiting said that couvade "should be a good index of [a] . . . wish to act out the feminine role and thus symbolically to be in part a woman" (1961:91). Individual expressions of feminin-ity are also possible. D'Andrade (1962) found that in the United States feminine identification as measured by the Franck Drawing Completion Test was strongly related to father absence during the first two years of life. Carlsmith (1963) found that father-absent male students had some feminine patterns on scholastic aptitude tests, an individual expression of cognitive cross-sex identity.

Since American society lacks a cultural mechanism such as circumcision at adolescence to overcome any conflict between primary feminine identity and secondary masculine identity (Whiting, Kluckhohn, and Anthony, 1958), neither a reaction against nor an expression of cross-sex identity is assured. Therefore, both are possible since there are wide variations in family types in the United States.

In general, then, the literature of psychological anthropology, particularly studies done by Whiting and his associates, has linked father absence and household types to primary sex identity in a causal relationship and has viewed certain sex-linked cultural phenomena, such as couvade and initiation rites, as results. In addition, certain behaviors, such as protest masculinity, have been said to be accounted for since presumed effects on individuals are said to explain the association of cultural events with household types. However, the actual connection between cross-sex identity and individual behavior has largely been assumed. Therefore, the study reported here sought to assess directly the usefulness of cross-sex identity for predicting individual expressions of femininity or protest masculinity.

The proposition that sex-role identity can, at least in part, account for these behaviors or, more generally, for errors in sex-role behavior is the basic notion we set out to test. Are these feminine and exaggeratedly masculine behaviors indeed expressions of or reactions to cross-sex identity? The answer has theoretical as well as practical implications—theoretical because the previously discussed explanations of cultural events hinge on the existence of a link between individual behavior and cross-sex identity; practical because if further research shows that errors in sex-role behavior in our society are in part functions of the early childhood factors and therefore errors in sex-role learning, "then they can be countered either by decreasing the exclusiveness of the early mother-child relationship, increasing the authority of the father during childhood, or instituting a formal means of coping with adolescent boys functionally equivalent to [male initiation rites]" (Whiting, Kluckhohn, and Anthony, 1958:370).

Before talking more specifically about these behaviors, we should examine the psychological literature on the subject of identification.

Psychological Theories of Identification

The following discussion of identification is limited to the range of problems relevant to this study and its anthropological antecedents. It may well appear naive and oversimplified to a psychologist. But as Devons and Gluckman point out:

. . . any social scientist has to confine what he studies within certain limits: he cannot include the whole of complex reality. This limitation is vital if his study is to be manageable. With the limitation goes simplification, which also seems necessary in order to isolate what appear to be the essential features under examination. (1964:16–17)

The concept of identification can, of course, be traced to Freud, but what Freud meant by identification varied in his writings. He mingled two definitions: copying and emotional ties (White, 1963:99). Recently Kagan has written:

The concept of identification is, to some degree, controversial. There is disagreement as to its usefulness in explaining aspects of human development, and even among those who regard the concept as fruitful there is no unanimity as to its definition. A major point of disagreement revolves around the question, to what events or processes does this term refer? (1964:146)

To Whiting (Whiting, Kluckhohn, and Anthony, 1958), identification is an emotional tie or involvement with another. Other writers view identification almost entirely as imitation (for example, White, 1963). Whiting made his position clear in 1960 (Maccoby, 1959, makes a similar point) by distinguishing between role learning and role performance. Whiting argued that while a child may learn a number of roles (imitation), he does not have an equal desire to perform them. *The wish to perform a role* is a function of identification with the person who ordinarily performs that role. As Roger Brown puts it, "our minds are full of other people but they do not all matter in equal degree" (1965:399). Implicit in the notion of identification then is motivation. Therefore, in this report, we shall define *identification* as *a process of imitation probably motivated by emotional ties to particular models.* An emotional tie without imitation is not identification here, although it would be to Whiting; neither is imitation without an emotional tie. There are many possible reasons for a child's imitation of behavior. Novelty, for example, is often sufficient cause for imitation, but "novelty alone will not serve to account for the acquisition of morality or superego" (Brown, 1965). We are, after all, talking about something more pervasive, around which much learning is organized. To Kagan, identification "is a belief that some of the attributes of a model belong to the self" (1964:146), a definition that at least implies an emotional tie (model) as well as imitation (belong to the self).

Yet what processes determine who the model is? There seem to be two major answers which try to specify the nature of the emotional tie that determines whom the child selects for his model:

1. The child is said to identify with the nurturant figure, the one who rewards him, and reinforces appropriate behavior. This opinion, shared by Sears, Rau, and Alpert (1966) and Cumming and Cumming (1962), among others, holds that motivation for imitation comes

from reinforcement of imitated behaviors, rewards, interaction, and the nurturant relationship in general.

2. The second position relates to Whiting's theory (Whiting, 1960) that the child identifies with the figure in control of the resources he needs, hence the motivation is "status envy."

Whiting, himself, believes that the primary cause of the wish to perform a role is envy of the person who ordinarily performs it. Whiting's theory is that a child will envy the status of another person when that person has "more efficient control over resources than he has" (Whiting 1960). Resources are anything the child desires: food, love, cars, dogs, etc. (Brown 1965:399)

Thus in matrifocal households the child would identify with women, leading, for boys, to cross-sex identity. However, two different types of status positions have been distinguished (although not by Whiting): (1) The child will identify with the *consumer* of resources that he himself needs (one kind of status envy). (2) The child will identify with the *controller* of the resources that he himself needs. This person controls who gets the resources and need not consume them himself to be envied. Bandura, Ross, and Ross performed the classic experiment dealing with these two alternatives. Children were found to identify more often with a controller of resources than with a consumer. Yet, as Brown states:

In Whiting's discussion these two things are not distinguished and, indeed, they often go together in life. When they are separated the Bandura experiment shows that it is power that attracts imitation. Perhaps this is because power reliably implies the possibility of enjoying resources while the enjoyment does not so reliably imply control over them. (1965:401)

This book will sidestep the problem of whether the child identifies with the nurturant figure or a person whose status he envies, a problem which has been investigated by many workers (see, for example, Bandura,

1962; Bandura, Ross, and Ross, 1963; Mussen and Distler, 1959; Sears, Rau, and Alpert, 1966). Regardless of whether it is the nurturant or controlling figure that is identified with, there is agreement that it is a *significant* figure.

Development of Sex Identity

The psychological literature distinguishes two kinds of sex identity: primary or "anaclitic" and secondary or "defensive." According to Sears, Rau, and Alpert:

Anaclitic identification is understood to be a mechanism, developed during the first three or four years of life, by which behaving like the parents — or perceiving the similarity between the self and the parents — becomes intrinsically rewarding. . . . The secondary form of identification (Freud, 1923) is conceived to be a defensive process in which the already established anaclitic identification produces an internalization of the punitive and restrictive qualities of a threatening parent; Freud limited his exploration of the process to its development in the boy, and hence emphasized the boy's threatening father. This kind of identification is a defense in the sense that it reduces the anxiety engendered in the boy by his own Oedipal hostilities. (1966:3–7)

It is clear that when Whiting and his associates speak of primary or "optative" sex identity they are talking about nearly the same thing as Sears' "anaclitic" sex identification (although Whiting and Sears disagree about how the model is chosen). The primary sex identity is presumably *unconscious,* while the secondary is quite conscious and almost studied.

It is assumed here that the primary sex identity remains throughout life, and that primary cross-sex identity for boys represents a cognitive pattern of femininity. Both the expression of feminine traits and the reaction of protest or exaggerated masculinity, therefore, can have an underlying feminine cognitive structure, and it is the secondary or conscious sex identity which varies, feminine in the former case, masculine in the latter.

Other writers prefer to call secondary identification "sex preference" and limit the word "identification" to what is here "primary sex identity" (D. G. Brown, 1956). Whatever the labels, primary sex identity is said to be an intrinsic cognitive style which cannot be changed, only covered over by later conscious influences. Kagan, in contrast to Brown, seems to use "sex identity" to refer to what is here called "secondary sex identity," for he defines sex-role identity as the degree to which a person describes himself as masculine or feminine (1964:144). Such a description would, of course, be based on one's conscious self-image and relates to Whiting's "subjective" identity discussed previously.

Having specified what we mean by "sex identity" and related our position and that of Whiting and his associates to psychological theories concerning identification and sex identity, we now turn to an examination of sexual differentiation and sex roles.

Sex-Role Differentiation

In 1936, Ralph Linton pointed out that "the division and ascription of statuses with relation to sex seems to be basic in all social systems. All societies prescribe different attitudes and activities to men and to women" (1936:116). D'Andrade (1966) reported evidence of some regularity in these assignments. There may be a persistent division of labor between men and women that assigns socio-emotional or integrative activities to women and instrumental activities to men. The female role has been described as diffuse integrative watchfulness, the male role as primarily striving toward a distant goal in spite of interruptions and obstacles. It is the woman who manages tension in the home, and the man who provides resources and opportunities. The woman's adult role in the home is generally particularistic, socio-emotional, and passive. The man's adult role is uni-

versalistic and instrumental, an active striving toward
goals which are often self-determined (see Parsons and
Bales, 1955; Lopata, 1965).

Yet societies vary in degree of sexual differentiation
(see, for example, Barry, Bacon, and Child, 1957) and
in the specific role sets assigned to the sexes (see, for
example, Mead, 1935). We are concerned in this book
with contemporary North American culture. According to
Kagan (1964), normal sexual differentiation in the United
States requires inhibition of verbal and physical aggression among girls and women but gives boys and men
license—and even encouragement—to express aggression when attacked, threatened, or dominated by another male. During socialization girls are allowed
greater license to express dependency, passivity, and
conformity; boys are pressured to inhibit these tendencies.

In sum, females are supposed to inhibit aggression, and open
display of sex urges, to be passive with men, to be nurturant
with others . . . and maintain an effective, socially poised, and
friendly posture with others. Males are urged to be aggressive
in face of attack, independent in problem situations, sexually
aggressive, in control of repressive urges, and suppressive of
strong emotion, especially anxiety.* (Kagan, 1964:140–141)

Specific components of the role sets may be present or
absent in individual cases. Mixtures, of course, are possible and probably normal. In given situations, men often
need socio-emotional skills; women sometimes need to
be instrumentally competent, particularly if the spouse is
absent from the home for periods of time. This may explain why over-differentiation as well as under-differ-

---

* This is not to say that boys cannot be anxious. Anxiety *per se*
may have nothing to do with sex role, but may rather be a part
of the human condition. Important to sex role is how anxiety
is expressed—for example by withdrawal or destructiveness.

entiation is considered deviant. Men and women must have internalized what the complementary role is, so that if necessary they *may* play it. However, our primary interest here is in the role the individual chooses to perform regularly.

Most studies suggest that sex-role learning begins early, probably at birth. To test the notion that behavioral expectations are differentiated sexually even at birth, Elaine Cumming classed names according to their implications for behavior. She found that girls' names were more particularistic and many were unique (for example, Darla, Elmina, Facene, Gayla, Hestine, Jacque, Jancy, Jerralyn, Jodyne, Joella, Karlen, Kendra, Krist, and LaDonna); she concluded: "It seems to be clear that girls do have more individual or expressive and particularistic names and boys more traditional and universalistic ones" (Cumming, 1966). Sears, Rau, and Alpert suggest:

. . . the ascription of a particular gender label at birth initiates a complex set of treatments (by the parents and siblings and various others) that establishes the attitudes, feelings, interests, tastes, mannerisms, traits, and habit structures characterizing children of that gender in the particular culture in which the child's rearing occurs. (1966:171)

Naming and sex-typing then begin the long process of differential expectation by which the sex roles are taught and through which socialization occurs.

The desired result of this socialization is that behavior of boys will be different from that of girls. This aim does, in fact, seem to be achieved. Hattwick (1937) long ago asked teachers to rate *normal* nursery school children on 60 behavior items. The teachers described the boys as aggressive toward other children, negative toward adults, and as exhibiting marked physical activity. They also had poor work habits, more speech difficulties, and a greater incidence of masturbation than girls. The girls were more likely to withdraw, give in too easily, avoid playing with others, stay near adults, be jealous, avoid risks, tell fanciful stories, and cry easily. They also had a greater tendency to twist their hair, refuse food, and boss others. Most of these differences were as obvious in a child of two as in a child of four, and most, with certain obvious exceptions, seem related to our description of adult male and female sex roles. Boys are more active, aggressive, outgoing; girls withdraw into a clique, avoid others, and are emotional. Beller and Neubauer (1963) found support for Hattwick. Boys were observed to exhibit hyperaggression, hyperactivity, and speech disturbances. Girls were more often reported to be overly dependent and lacking in emotional control. Note again that boys, while active and aggressive, have trouble with verbal skills, which are more crucial to the feminine role.

Vener and Snyder (1966) found that children two and one-half to five years old could accurately identify sex linkage of various artifacts, attesting to the early age at which children learn sex-role behavior. Further, a high level of agreement with adult judges suggests a high intergenerational stability for this particular measure. Rabban (1950) found that boys were clearly more aware than girls of sex-appropriate behavior in the choice of toys; however, Vener and Snyder (1966) found no differences between boys and girls in ability to identify sex linkage of artifacts. They did find that *both* did better with female-linked artifacts, suggesting that the female role is incorporated first. A direct test with their data bears this out for boys. The youngest boys, aged two and one-half had a slight preference for feminine items, but this was completely corrected by the boys aged five. Hetherington (1965), however, found that girls developed preference for their sex role at a later age than boys.

Goodenough (1957) found that boys had greater need to show sex-appropriate behavior and were oriented toward the environment, displaying sociability, aggressiveness, obstinacy, and emotional suppression. Girls were personally oriented: pliable, submissive, gentle, emotional, sensitive, and likely to court affection.

Differences in children's behavior are not surprising in light of studies of parents. Most parents punish aggression and open sexuality more consistently in daughters than in sons. They punish passivity, dependency, and open display of fear more consistently in sons than in daughters (Kagan, 1964:151; see, for example, Aberle and Naegele, 1952; Kohn, 1959; Sears, Maccoby, and Levin, 1957).

Although aggressiveness has often been found more characteristic of boys before six than of girls (Beller and Neubauer, 1963; Dawe, 1934; Green, 1933; Hartup and Himino, 1959; Jersild and Markey, 1935; McCandless, Bilous, and Bennett, 1961; Moore and Ucko, 1961; Sears, Pintler, and Sears, 1946; Walters, Pearce, and Dahms, 1957), some investigators have found the difference to be that boys are more likely to aggress physically while girls are more likely to aggress verbally (Durrett, 1959; Vroegh and Handridge, 1966). Muste and Sharpe (1947) found that boys grabbed to initiate aggression and used physical resistance as a response. Girls used all types of verbal techniques both in initiating aggression and in responding. The means by which aggression is expressed and its object, rather than aggression *per se*, are therefore important.

It should also be pointed out that many of the studies here reported were done in experimental or artificial group settings, and were not based upon observation of children in their normal behavioral setting. This limitation has an unknown effect on the role sets as here described.

The conclusions we draw from this child-development literature are the following:

1. Cross-cultural accounts of sexual differentiation are confirmed and elaborated in studies of child behavior in the United States.

2. These studies demonstrate that sex-role learning is

accomplished early and that normally both sex roles are learned by each individual.

3. Identification is said to account at least in part for the predisposition to choose one sex role over the other.

Now we turn to an examination of the relationship between sex identity and errors in sex-role behavior.

II. ERRORS IN SEX-ROLE BEHAVIOR

This study examined the link between sex identity and the two principal types of errors in sex-role behavior among adolescent boys: uncontrolled or exaggeratedly masculine behavior and inappropriate sex-role, or feminine, behavior.* The study population, made up of boys with socio-psychological problems, was divided into three groups: boys with exaggeratedly masculine behavior, boys with inappropriate sex-role behavior, and a control group of boys who evinced neither error in sex-role behavior but had other behavior problems or intrapsychic or physical problems.

Within the framework of sex roles in American society, boys whose behavior is considered appropriate to the

---

* John Whiting suggests that these errors in sex-role behavior could be viewed as a strong preference for either sex role, suggesting that for the United States normal boys ought not choose between sex roles but perform aspects of both (Whiting, personal communication). Suttles' (1968) material would suggest that this is true only of the upper range of the class spectrum. Sexual differentiation is great among slum dwellers, and may stand in inverse relationship with class.

17

male role but exaggerated or uncontrolled are said to be overly active, aggressive, loud, belligerent, independent, and destructive. Excerpts from an interview with the mother of a boy in the group with exaggeratedly masculine behavior follow. The behavior described in this randomly chosen example is typical of the boys in this group:

Q.* We were having many problems with him and sought private psychiatric care. [They couldn't afford it and so went to a clinic.] I told them I wanted to avoid serious trouble. Q. Now last February Joe stayed home alone for two to three weeks when we were in a bad car accident. We were all badly injured, and spent two to three weeks in the hospital. We were home a week when the state trooper shows up asking for Joe's boots. . . . Joe had broken into the country club, stole a golf cart, and took it on a joy ride. . . . He ended up on a year's probation.

Q. Joe seems to resent all authority. Joe does what Joe wants to do. Rules are made for other people not me. He broke purposefully every rule and regulation in school. For example, he went to a football game after school, called, said he was bloody . . . he got in a fight and had beaten the other kid with brass knuckles. You know the reason? Because the kid was wearing white socks and Joe didn't like them.

Q. He threatened me with an ax because I told him he couldn't do something. He was caught with a switchblade knife. . . . There was no disciplining him at home at all . . . car, car, car . . . that's all . . . he's wanted to drive my car since he was fourteen.

Q. He would beat up his brothers as the only way to beat me up. He failed school three years in a row. He has three letters in sports though, soccer, football, and baseball. He has a steady girlfriend. . . . He had one girl at fifteen who was eighteen. I insisted they break up.

Q. In the last year Joe has been drinking very heavily [he is now sixteen]. A lot of the times he has lost control we think

* A Q. means a question was asked or a probe was made by the interviewer. The reader is referred to the appendix for a copy of the interview for use as an outline.

he may have been drunk. *Q.* Once wanted the car and told his father to give him the keys or he'd take a sledge hammer to it. They really went at it [verbally]. *Q.* He's always making wisecracks in school. He considers only himself, is a chronic liar, and swears.

The second group of boys are those who have chosen to imitate the inappropriate sex role. These boys generally inhibit verbal and physical aggression, while expressing dependency, passivity, conformity, withdrawal, and emotion. It should be pointed out that by "inappropriate sex-role behavior" we do not mean homosexuality. Homosexuality is here viewed as an independent behavior cluster which is neither clearly exaggerated masculinity nor inappropriate sex-role behavior. In fact it may be both. Ferenczi (1914) distinguished between passive homosexuals who feel as women and active homosexuals who feel as men. Cutter (1964) did link primary cross-sex identity with aggressive homosexuality, but preference for sexual relations with members of one's own biological sex can probably arise from a number of different situations. At any event, homosexuality should not be assumed or inferred from our term "inappropriate sex-role behavior." If someone is described as a passive or an active homosexual, he will be interesting to us primarily because of the words "passive" and "active." Furthermore, for the age group we will consider in this study—thirteen to nineteen—it is not clear whether homosexual behavior is abnormal in a statistical sense. Kinsey and his associates (1948) found that homosexual experience in adolescence is not uncommon.

A description of a boy from the group with behavior inappropriate to the male role follows, again excerpts from an interview with his mother:

Q. We applied because last summer, sometime in July, we noticed for quite a while that Bill was terribly withdrawn and needed help. We talked it over with the family physician, and

he suggested the county mental health clinic, and a psychiatrist there recommended hospitalization for fifteen days, and he went to . . . [Agency 1] and he didn't cooperate too well. Q. He wouldn't socialize in general. He wanted to be discharged and registered for school. When released, he didn't want to go. We let him stay, thinking he would snap out of it. He had days when he would never speak. . . .
    Q. Truthfully, he never gave any trouble to anyone at all. I have three older sons and they were rough and ready. Bill was quiet and a homebody. He was quiet, never aggressive, and had few friends. Q. He liked school, although he was a slow learner. . . . He passed but in high school failed a couple. He would have been a senior last year. Q. No, he didn't care at all for sports, only basketball, and that not ardently. Q. Most of the time he goes to movies and parks. Q. In the past year there has been a definite change. Q. He has become more withdrawn. He was always devoted to me, I think too devoted. I'd like to see him get a girl, have an affair. He likes girls but makes no effort to date them.

All the boys not classified as above comprised the third group, the controls, who did not exhibit errors in sex-role behavior, but had other types of problems. Some were simply immature or had intrapsychic problems (paranoia, depression, leveled affect) or problems resulting from physical disorders (brain damage, cerebral palsy). A randomly chosen description of the behavior of a boy in the control group follows:

    Q. Doug was certified in New York City, went into Bellevue under apparently LSD, he denied his relatives' existence and was certified. We had him transferred . . . [to Agency 4]. He is now home [after being in the hospital for more than a month].
    Q. Doug's a pretty good kid. Would you expect any other answer? His interests are strictly creative. He couldn't care less for the absolute sciences. He's moody, introverted. Q. Now he is [popular] with his own society. I don't know. I think he is quite popular. Q. He has won several art contests, is now working in a foundry. [Ironic laugh.] He has quite a lot of friends, some I don't even know. Even when a little kid,

when he got in scraps, he wouldn't talk about it. He's not an introvert, but not an extrovert. Everyone knows and likes him. He went to military school. It didn't seem to work. He flunked courses, but with cramming passed the regents.

Q. . . . He likes sports very much, good at baseball and lacrosse . . . his smoking interfered, he wanted to play football but was too small. *Q.* When in the eighth grade, he had to go in and have his lymph glands taken out. We thought he had rheumatic fever, and he was sick a long time. He had several illnesses and missed school. He had always been very top scholastically. From that point, he seemed determined to get stature by being a goof-off. He missed beginning football practice — from that point on seemed to only channel his efforts into things he was interested in. From these sorts of things I guess Michaelangelos spring. To cope with the creative mind is a tough proposition.

Q. Two or three days after he was eighteen, he got two or three more beers than he could handle, the police picked him up with a kid who'd been in trouble before. He was AWOL from military school because he'd had enough [parents seem proud]. Said to us, "I'm the Catcher in the Rye." He calls himself an existentialist and takes what he reads seriously. He went down to New York to visit a girl, and he called us and asked his father if he could stay in Greenwich Village. He said all right. Somewhere, somehow he got tangled up with this pot and LSD crowd. He was living in the same building with that poet Greenberg . . . [Ginsberg?]. As it has a thousand and one other people, Greenwich Village whipped him. It's a cesspool.

On the basis of the theories discussed in Chapter 1, we would expect the boys with exaggeratedly masculine behavior to have primary cross-sex identity and secondary male identity and to have had fathers absent early in life, but present later. Similarly, we would expect boys with inappropriate sex-role behavior to have both primary and secondary cross-sex identity and fathers absent both early and late. Controls would be expected to have normally male primary and secondary identity. But it is necessary to test these expectations.

Previous Research

Many scholars have investigated the link between sex identity and behavior, but never for these groupings. As mentioned previously, B. Whiting (1965) explained male aggression as "protest masculinity," and found that it was more prevalent in those societies in which the father is of little importance to the infant, but has high status later in the child's life. Munroe, Munroe, and Whiting (1965) found hypermasculinity present in those individuals whose couvade activity was the strongest, evidence that "underlying psychological femininity . . . [can be] accompanied by defensive masculinity at the overt level of role performance." Munroe found, first in a cross-cultural study (n.d.) and later in a study of the Black Carib of British Honduras (1964), that the couvade could be interpreted as an expression of cross-sex identity, and that strength of couvade practice was significantly correlated with father absence and matrilocal extended family structure. Whiting, Kluckhohn, and Anthony (1958) viewed juvenile delinquency in the United States as indicative of defensive masculinity; as suggested earlier, such a reaction typically comes about when a male child with primary feminine identity develops secondary masculine identity. Mussen and Distler (1959) found that boys with strong secondary male identification had warm relationships with their fathers, a perception of the father as nurturant, and more masculine behavior and attitudes. Webb (1963) found that boys and girls with strong secondary feminine identification had superior school attendance records.

Errors in sex-role behavior seem to be somewhat refractory to treatment. As Sears pointed out:

So far as the strength of the role behavior is concerned, witness the difficulty of therapeutic modification of male character disorders that include severe passivity, or the intransigence of gender roles in pseudohermaphrodites. (Sears, Rau, and Alpert, 1966:171)

Kagan and Moss (1962) found in their longitudinal study that boys who were passive during the first ten years of life adopted non-masculine interests as adults. The association was significant even when passivity during the first three years was the predictor. Passivity among boys six to ten also predicted inappropriate sex-role behavior in adulthood (Kagan and Moss, 1962:200–201). In addition, boys who are aggressive to their mothers between the ages of three and ten can be expected to be aggressive in adulthood.

A recent longitudinal study by Robins (1966) has shown that sociopathy, schizophrenia, and hysteria are relatively more frequent in an adult population that had visited a child guidance clinic in adolescence. Behaviors usually associated with these disorders would often be either exaggeratedly male or inappropriate to the male role. Manic-depressives and neurotics (who would be classed as controls in this report) were not found as often among those adults who had been labeled "deviant" in adolescence. This is presumptive evidence that *errors in sex-role behavior are relatively persistent throughout the life cycle* and these findings indicate some support for the relative permanence of these styles of behavior.*

---

* Kagan and Moss found that "When a behavior is congruent with the traditional definition of sex appropriate behavior, it is likely to be predictive of phenotypically similar behavior in adulthood. When it conflicts with traditional sex-role standards, the relative motive is more likely to find behavioral expression in derivative or substitute responses that are socially more acceptable. . . . passivity . . . did not predict passivity or dependence but did predict theoretically reasonable derivatives (non-competitiveness, non-masculine interests, social anxiety and avoidance of sexuality)" (1962:200). This finding is congruent with the theory presented here because these are still inappropriate sex-role behaviors, and *represent a continued pattern of inappropriate sex-role behavior.* The difference is merely that in a child passivity is noticed, while in an adult avoidance of sexuality is noticed. The person is, however, still behaving inappropriately to his sex role.

Lipsitt and Strodtbeck (1967), in a study closely related to this book but published after this research was
completed, classified male subjects into sex-role identity
types based on their scores on two tests of masculinity-
femininity. Following Lansky (1964; 1965), Lipsitt and
Strodtbeck view the Franck Drawing Completion Test
as a measure of primary (unconscious) sex identity, and
the Gough Femininity Scale as a measure of secondary
(conscious) sex identity. Using these two measures, they
classified subjects as one of four types (primary identity
is given first): masculine-masculine (MM), masculine-
feminine (MF), feminine-masculine (FM), and feminine-
feminine (FF). They found that in a simulated court
trial, FM subjects were more likely to find a defendant
guilty when homosexuality was ascribed to the defendant. FM subjects emphasized their own masculinity by dealing harshly with what the study viewed as
feminine traits in others. FF subjects were more likely
to find the defendant not guilty; that is, the FF subjects
"allowed the tangential issue of homosexuality to direct
them toward a *not guilty* finding" (Lipsitt and Strodtbeck, 1967).

Hypotheses of the Study

This study tests four hypotheses relating errors in sex-
role behavior to sex identity:

Hypothesis 1: Boys who are labeled "deviant" for exaggeratedly male behavior or for behavior inappropriate
to the male role will have greater primary cross-sex
identity than boys who are not thus labeled "deviant."

Hypothesis 2: Boys labeled "deviant" for inappropriate
sex-role behavior will have greater secondary cross-
sex identity than either the boys labeled "exaggeratedly
male" or the boys not labeled "deviant" in terms of
their sex-role behavior (controls).

Since sleeping arrangements in American society are fairly uniformly man and wife in the same room, the relevant concern relating to father absence is not whether the infant sleeps with the mother but whether or not the father is present in the house. Thus, his presence or absence would be significant for both primary and secondary sex identity. Father absence, said to lead to cross-sex identification in the Whiting material, has been linked directly with lack of aggressiveness in doll play (Bach, 1946; Sears, Pintler, and Sears, 1946), difficulty in establishing peer relations (Lynn and Sawrey, 1958), and relative lack of mathematical skills on scholastic aptitude tests (Carlsmith, 1963). Since boys typically do better than girls at mathematical reasoning and problem solving (see, for example, Milton, 1957; Herzberg and Lepkin, 1954; Kostick, 1954), the association of lack of skill in mathematical analysis with father absence in boys is inferential evidence for the cross-sex identity theories outlined above. Hetherington (1965) has linked father absence to withdrawn, passive behavior in boys. Howe (1966) linked father absence and later exclusive male associations with boisterous group drinking behavior and aggression. Father absence has previously been linked with lack of aggressiveness, but the timing of the father absence in the child's life has not been examined previously. Therefore, our study was designed to test the following hypothesis:

Hypothesis 3: The families of boys with behavior inappropriate to the male role will be marked by father absence. Boys with exaggeratedly male behavior will have experienced father absence in early childhood, followed by some male influence in later childhood.

As discussed in Chapter 1, we think that imitation is a part of identification. Therefore, as a check on our hypotheses linking sex-role identity with adolescent errors in sex-role behavior, we may also ask whom the child imitates. Boys reported deviant for exaggeratedly male behavior would be expected to perform typically male tasks at home—that is, share more tasks with their fathers than with their mothers. Boys reported deviant for behavior inappropriate to the male role would be expected to share more tasks with their mothers than with their fathers. The exact content of the tasks is unimportant here. Thus our last hypothesis is:

Hypothesis 4: Boys with exaggeratedly male behavior will share more household tasks with their fathers, and boys with inappropriate sex-role behavior will share more household tasks with their mothers.

Positive results on this hypothesis will help substantiate any differences in actual "conscious sex-identity" that we find. Further, such findings would help substantiate our use of the concept of sex roles to classify the behaviors we are dealing with, for they would show that even relative to *a particular family's definition* of which tasks are male and which female, not just to some societal standard, boys with exaggeratedly male behavior choose male tasks, while boys with inappropriate sex-role behavior choose female tasks.

Social Class and Biological Factors

Two variables seemed likely to confound our findings and therefore had to be controlled. Social class has been linked to aggression, which is a large component of the exaggeratedly male behaviors. Biological factors have been linked to the active-passive dimension, which is an important one in distinguishing exaggeratedly male from inappropriate sex-role behavior.

Social class and aggression

Several studies have shown that aggressiveness is more characteristic of lower-class males than of middle-class males in the United States. For example, Fannin and Clinard (1965) found that lower-class boys conceived of themselves as tougher, more fearless, more powerful, fiercer, and more dangerous than middle-class boys. They more often carried weapons and committed violent offenses. Among lower-class households, the instances of father absence can also be expected to be more numerous than among middle-class or upper-class households (see Udry, 1966). Therefore, the theory outlined previously would account for the association between social class and aggression by the cross-sex identity resulting from father absence (Whiting, Kluckhohn, and Anthony, 1958).

However, it is also possible that greater aggression in lower-class males is a response to their position in the larger society or normal behavior in a subculture of poverty, related more to frustration than to cross-sex identity. Therefore, an association between aggression and social class cannot be *assumed* to support our hypotheses. *The greater incidence of broken homes among the lower class may in fact lead us to find a spurious relationship between cross-sex identity and exaggeratedly male behavior.* For this reason, it is important that we remove the purely social class effect when examining our hypotheses.

Biological factors

Kagan and Moss report that there is "some beginning evidence suggesting that the constitutional differences between males and females may be associated with an active-passive behavioral continuum" (1962:81). Lacey and Lacey (1958) found college males with low cardiac

arrythmia scores to have slower reactions. Kagan and
Moss (1962) found passivity in childhood to be associated
with a minimal degree of spontaneous cardiac arrythmia
in adulthood.

The possibility of different androgen levels between
those boys whose behavior is exaggeratedly masculine
and those with inappropriate sex-role behavior is also
a real one. Perhaps the former have more male hormones
than the latter. In a related experiment, Gerall (1966)
found that prenatal androgen permanently modifies
the neural structures that integrate mating behavior in
female guinea pigs. Levine, reviewing the literature
in 1966, found increasing evidence that mammalian behavior patterns are basically female and that male patterns are induced by the action of the sex hormone tes-
tosterone on the brain of the newborn animal. However,
as far as secondary sex identity is concerned, the most recent review of research in transvestism, a most extreme
form of inappropriate sex-role behavior, found no evidence to support a biological etiology for the condition
(Housden, 1965). In view of the many social features
of sex-role behavior, this is not surprising; however,
the possible effect of body chemistry on the active-
passive dimension cannot be ruled out so easily. As
Money wrote:

Sex differences in the androgen-estrogen ratio may conceivably
account for some of the differences between men and women
in their thresholds for erotically related behavior and activity. In the male, for instance, there is typically a greater
expenditure of energy in the service of sexual searching,
pursuit, and consummation. This energy expenditure ex-
tends also to adventurous, exploratory roaming, to assertive-
ness and aggression and to the defense of territorial rights.
(1965:x)

There is no sure way to test these notions except by
complicated blood and urine tests, which were not pos-

sible in the present inquiry. Androgen levels are important to us primarily for their effect on energy levels, and while we could not examine androgen levels directly, we were able to obtain other approximations of energy and of physique. These will be discussed in the next chapter.

III. METHOD OF THE STUDY

The study population was composed of adolescent boys who appeared for help at mental health agencies serving a county in Upstate New York. Since they applied for aid, we can assume that they were considered deviant by their parents and community. Five mental health agencies handle the bulk of the disturbed adolescent boys in the county: two state mental hospitals, one state residential school for emotionally disturbed children, and two outpatient mental health clinics.

Each of these agencies was initially asked to furnish us the names and addresses of all boys aged thirteen to nineteen who applied for its services between June 1, 1966 and September 1, 1966. This method of collecting a cohort was intended to assure us of a representative sample of boys that would enable us to treat our results statistically. The estimates of case load provided us by the directors of these agencies assured that we would collect over one hundred names in a three-month period. However, as name-gathering progressed, it became apparent that the directors' estimates had been greatly exaggerated. The director of one agency, for example, estimated that one new adolescent boy a week

31

was seen; however, in the three months of the summer
of 1966 the agency served only one new boy. This is not
an isolated example. Personnel in all the agencies in the
study similarly overestimated the number of male
adolescents they were seeing by ratios of three or four
to one. This overestimate is probably related to the
fact that many of the boys are, to say the least, very active,
aggressive, and troublesome. The directors therefore
seem to feel that they treat more of them than they in
fact do (although it also has something to say about how
close the administrators are to the actual workings of
the hospital). Anyone who has acted as babysitter for an
overactive child will appreciate their misperception.

In any event, more names were needed, so the time
period for collecting new admissions was extended to
October 1, 1966. We also went back to January 1, 1965
to collect names of boys previously admitted for treatment. These methods were required in order to collect
the 133 names this study is based upon. We did not go
back further than January 1, 1965 because it became
more difficult to locate the boys the older the cases
were. Of the 133 names collected, it was impossible to
find 17 boys, and the bulk of these were the earlier
cases. The method of collecting the names varied with
each agency. The methods are explained below, along
with a brief description of each agency and its functioning.

Agency 1 is a small (50 bed) state mental hospital
serving the largest city in the county and situated near
the city's center. It provides inpatient and outpatient
treatment for those over sixteen. We distributed forms to
the intake workers of the hospital so they could record
current applicants for admission, and searched and abstracted the hospital's records for previous admissions
of males under twenty. Agency 1 furnished 10 names.
The families of 9 of these boys were interviewed, and
7 boys were tested. Two were not tested because one

was in jail at the time of testing and the mother of the other boy thought the testing would upset her nervous, paranoid boy.

Agency 2 is a Catholic mental health clinic, with an attached mental ward in a Catholic general hospital, serving all ages. In a letter, the parents of each of the boys served in the time period under consideration were asked if they were willing to participate in the study (the actual number is therefore unknown to us). If the parents responded favorably, the agency gave us the names and addresses of the boys. We could not search the agency's records and had no access to their files. The agency gave us only 5 names. The 5 families who said they would take part were interviewed and all 5 boys were tested.

Agency 3 is a state school for emotionally disturbed children located outside the county and on the grounds of Agency 4. It serves children up to age sixteen. Forms were distributed to the intake workers for recording current applications, and the records of the school were searched for the names and addresses of boys from our county admitted within the period of interest. The school records were abstracted for all cases. The children are enrolled in this school for the academic year and live at the school, going home (if they have a family) only for vacations, if they are sufficiently "improved." As the boys improve, vacations are also used as trial visits for those boys who are up for adoption. This school furnished the names of 18 boys. We were able to interview the families or foster families of 15, and these 15 boys were tested.

Agency 4 is a large (3600 bed) state mental hospital serving all ages. It is located outside the county but serves it as the closest large state hospital. It is attached to Agency 3, and both are 55 miles from the center of the study county. It has a large adolescent service for those too old for Agency 3 or those thought not suitable for school. Names of boys from our county were gathered as in Agency 3. We received 35 names, and 30 families were interviewed. Twenty-four of the boys were tested. Six were not tested for the following reasons: one was in jail, two were in state schools for juvenile offenders, one had run away, one was in a military hospital, and one was living alone and refused to be tested. In addition, two boys could be only partially tested; one was a deaf-mute and the other would take only the Franck Drawing Completion Test.

Agency 5 is a county mental health clinic serving children up to age sixteen. Names of boys applying for help between January 1965 and June 1966 were collected. (There were no current admissions because the agency had closed its intake due to lack of staff, the result of a low salary scale imposed by an economy-minded county government.) The parents were invited by letter to take part in the study. If they refused, as 11 did, their names were not available to us. Of the 65 boys whose names we received, we were able to locate and interview the families of 59. Of these, 51 boys were tested. Eight were not tested for the following reasons: three were in state schools for juvenile offenders, two were in jail, two were "away," and one refused to be tested. Records of the agency were then abstracted.

Table 3.1

Summary of the Sources of the Research Cohort

	Number of Names of Boys Received	Number for Whom Parents Were Inter-viewed	Per Cent of Boys Whose Parents Were Inter-viewed	Number of Boys Tested	Per Cent of Boys Tested	Per Cent Tested of Boys for Whom We Had Inter-views
Agency 1	10	9	88.8	7	70.0	77.7
Agency 2	5	5	100.0	5	100.0	100.0
Agency 3	18	15	83.3	15	83.3	100.0
Agency 4	35	30	85.7	24	68.5	80.0
Agency 5	65	59	90.7	51	78.4	86.4
	133	118	88.7	102	74.4	83.9

A summary of the sources of the cohort used in this study is given in Table 3.1.

Collection of Data on Behavior

When an anthropologist studies mental illness, he is concerned, not with how deviant individuals act in a laboratory or hospital, but with how they function in the community. As Solon Kimball put it: "The anthropologist uses the real life setting as his laboratory. It is his objective to . . . determine the characteristics of ongoing systems as they operate within a set of conditions" (personal communication). Given this orientation, it is not surprising that anthropologists have joined with those social psychiatrists who are attempting to reconceptualize "mental illness" in terms of its *social manifestations in the community*. The psychiatrist John Cumming writes:

Classifying mental illness according to the social actions of the . . . [mentally ill] is not new. In a sense, Kraepelin did this when he categorized patients according to their behavior in mental hospitals. Mental hospitals, however, make few demands on patients as far as task performance is concerned. . . . Furthermore, in hospitals, the staff often finds it convenient to limit the amount and variety of activity, especially goal-directed activity.

In such an artificially constricted situation, failures of task performance will not be prominent. Cumming continues:

At the same time, mental hospitals often provide an inadequate input of information and stimulation for their patients, and this deprivation probably predisposes them to disorders of thought and perception. It seems useful, therefore, to attempt a system of classification that will describe the patient's functioning in a more nearly natural milieu—the community. Ego failure probably cannot be fully understood independently of the scene of the failure, any more than a figure can be perceived independently of its ground. (Cumming 1963:723–724)

As Cumming points out, by focusing on behavior in its natural milieu one conceptualizes in ways different from those most widely in use. What is sought is a system for classifying the patient's *behavior* in a natural milieu — his own community — and what is needed is a theory that will predict that behavior. Various social symptoms (role failures) are available to use, such as, chronic unemployment, chronic marital instability, violence, and passivity. These are all behavior descriptions of the patient's normal functioning (out of hospital). Likewise, classification of the behavior of the "mentally ill" based on errors in sex-role behavior would be derived from socially relevant categories. This study then tests whether errors in sex-role behavior in a group of boys labeled mentally ill can be predicted by identification theory.

One condition imposed upon the researchers by the participating agencies — which flowed from recent federal regulations governing the rights of subjects and the risks of harming them — was that only standard psychological tests could be administered to the boys. It was agreed that the boys would not be interviewed, since it was considered that questioning them about their past or present behavior might be too upsetting and lead to situations which the interviewers were not competent or licensed to handle. Therefore, in our attempt to get data on the boys' behavior, we were restricted to interviews and observation of their families and abstracts of the agency's records of parental complaints when available.

We visited the family of each boy and talked with a parent, occasionally both but more usually the mother. We asked (1) why they had applied for help for their son, (2) what sorts of things he did that bothered them, and (3) what his normal behavior was, both in and out of the home, and we probed for some life-history material. Open-ended questions were utilized. After information about the boy's behavior was obtained, the subject of questioning switched to the family itself, the social class, and the composition of the household.

Certain hazards of dealing with so much material at one time will occur to the reader. Since the researcher was aware of the hypotheses at risk and was dealing with both independent variables (social class, household composition) and dependent variables (boy's behavior), the possibility of biased probing to substantiate the hypotheses existed. Two safeguards against this hazard were utilized. The first was the ordering of the interviews. The data on social class and household composition were collected only after all the child behavior material had been collected. Material on social class and household composition were thought less susceptible to biased probing than the child's behavior patterns would have been had questions about behavior come after the family background was known.

While solving some of the problems, this method was admittedly far from perfect. Therefore, the second safeguard was that half of the interviewing was done by *another* interviewer, one who was not informed of the specific hypotheses at risk. There are no significant differences in the main relationships reported in the findings of this book between the subjects of the two interviewers. We therefore are reassured that interviewer bias does not account for our results.

There was good agreement between the statements of parents in the interviews about the boys' behavioral problems and the agency records of complaints by parents. In only one case was there strong disagreement. The child had been referred by the court to the hospital for psychiatric evaluations, and despite the protests of the interviewer, the mother, who told us the child was an angel, believed that her answers would have an effect on his case in court. Therefore, the record was taken as more valid than the interview. In all other cases the records, when available, were only used to supplement the interview data.

Coding of data

After all the data had been collected, the boys' behaviors were coded as predominantly either exaggeratedly male (E), inappropriate to the male role (I), or control (C), which was behavior considered deviant but having nothing to do with sex role. If a predominantly E boy also demonstrated some I or C behaviors, for example, this was noted. Coding was done independently by the two interviewers. Agreement between them on the dominant patterns was good (reliability 89.8), and the minor patterns (with lower intercoder reliability) were dropped. Differences were all resolvable.

The population yielded behavior data for 48 E boys (40 were tested), 24 I boys (22 were tested), 25 C boys (21 were tested), and 21 boys with equally prevalent exaggeratedly male and inappropriate sex-role behavior (EI) (18 were tested).

In terms of age, the cohort was well distributed (Table 3.2). E boys tend to be younger than any of the other groups, but the meaning of this is unclear. E be-

Table 3.2

Age Distribution of Groups E, I, and C

Group	N	Age 12–14	15–16	17–19
E	48	26	14	8
I	24	8	10	6
C	25	9	10	6
EI	21	5	10	6
Totals	118	48	44	26 *

* Reflects the fact that Agencies 3 and 5 took no one over sixteen.

Testing that E boys are younger than all others, $X^2 = 5.2$, d.f. = 1, $P < .05$.

haviors are of course the most impinging and perhaps the first noticed. Age does not affect our findings, however. The main findings in Chapter 4 were all run with age controlled; it had no effect on their significance. The age distribution of the entire sample is a function of the age restrictions of the individual agencies.

The *EI* group of boys was reexamined. The existence of a group of boys (21 in number) who strongly exhibited both exaggeratedly male and inappropriate sex-role behaviors should have been expected. Typically these boys were reported as usually being quiet, withdrawn, and passive, but occasionally exploding into rages, and so forth. Whereas they were aggressive to people and things (an *E* characteristic), the aggression was never planned and was very often *verbal*. It seemed to be a hysterical striking out at anything near. We decided that this was actually *uncontrolled emotion*, an *I* trait, and these youths were therefore reclassified as predominantly *I*. (If the reader is unable to accept this rationalization, he should know that all statistical analyses were also carried out with the *EI* group removed from the *I* group. No differences were found in the results.)

Much more striking, of course, was to discover twice as many *E* and *I* boys as controls. This will be discussed in the next chapter.

Instruments Used

Measures of father absence and household composition

The household history of the child from birth was collected in order to find out who had been around him as he grew up. A way to elicit this data was needed that would help the parent remember the past without requiring an endless number of questions. A sheet called "The History of the Household of the Child" was devised with these objectives in mind (see Appendix). It lists the possible members of the household down the

left side, and years of age in squares across the page,
running from birth to the present. A line is drawn through
the squares indicating the period each family member
was present. For example, if the father was away at
birth, came in when the subject was two, and left when
the subject was sixteen, a line is drawn from two to sixteen for Father. The household is defined as where the
child is, so there is no space allotted to the subject since
he is always present. Institutions are given a line at the
bottom of the page. If a line is drawn there, there will,
of course, be no other line on the page for that period.

The instrument provided an easy way to record a
wealth of data. The mother could watch as the sheet was
filled out, since its purpose and workings could be explained to her. She was often able to add things she had
previously forgotten, as well as to correct the interviewer when he misunderstood what she said.

The fault with this method of collecting the household history of the child is that the data is of doubtful
validity. The Fels study showed poor recollection by
subjects of this sort of longitudinal data (Jerome Kagan,
personal communication). Memory lapses, wish fantasies, and withholding of facts render this method subject to severe question. This will be discussed further
in Chapter 5.

Measure of sharing of household tasks

In order to determine how the boys' household activities overlap with those of other family members,
we chose an instrument designed by Ferraro and Turner
(n.d.) which asks who performs simple tasks around the
house. The tasks are listed down the page vertically on
the left, and the members of the household are arrayed
across the page to the right (see Appendix). Whether
someone performs a certain task sometimes, usually, or
always was recorded. Then *any* overlaps in tasks between a boy and his mother and father were counted.
The number of overlaps for mother minus the number for

father yielded a score representing numbers of tasks. The higher the score, the more tasks were shared with the mother. Negative scores indicate more overlap with the father. If the father was absent from the household it was impossible to compute a score. If he had been replaced, the overlap with the stepfather was utilized.

Measures of sex identity

The Franck Drawing Completion Test consists of 36 incomplete drawings that have been found to be completed differently by men and women. The subject is instructed to complete the drawings "any way it seems most fun." By the application of seven principles (closure, expansion, internal elaboration, angularity, unity, reliance upon a single line, and content), each completed drawing is scored as characteristically male or female. Female drawings are then scored 1, and male drawings 0, and the higher the total score, the more feminine the subject's primary sex identity.

The validity of the Franck Test has been demonstrated by significant differences between mean scores of men and women (Franck, n.d.; Franck and Rosen, 1949). McElroy (1954) demonstrated that males made more angular, closed designs and females more open, rounded designs, which agrees with the Franck scoring system. No effort, however, has been made to demonstrate the repeatability of the test if the same subject were to retake it. The test has been used often in studies of sex identity (Lansky, 1965), but with varying degrees of success because the scoring is complex and requires some training.

There are many scoring principles, and considerable differences of interpretation are possible. A complex scoring instruction sheet, which is fairly reliable, has been devised (Franck, n.d.) and revised (Lansky, 1959). In published reports agreement between scorers has been relatively high. Reliability ran from .84 to .90 (Meadows, 1959). In order to achieve this, however, scorers should have had experience with the test and should be trained in scoring techniques.

Since the researcher had not had extensive experience in scoring the Franck Test, the following procedure was adopted. Each test, identified only by a case number, was scored by the researcher. Then the tests were scored independently by a biostatistician trained by the researcher in scoring techniques. Reliability was 83.3 per cent. Differences were then resolved. The tests were then mailed to an educational psychologist with extensive experience in scoring the Franck Test. She scored them independently as a check on the previous scoring. Her scoring agreed 88.6 per cent of the time with the revised scores. The tests were then reviewed by the researcher and the biostatistician in order to reconcile the differences with the scoring of the educational psychologist. All differences were able to be resolved to our mutual satisfaction except for a group that resulted from a difference in interpretation of two of the scoring rules. The judgment of the educational psychologist was accepted in these cases, since she was the more experienced scorer.

The Franck Test is assumed to measure unconscious shapes and styles of design which have been found to be typical of men or women. It tests unconscious or primary sex identity, for there is no possibility of a conscious choice to be male or female entering into its results. Further support for this assumption comes from Katz (1959), whose preliminary study of responses of children to the Franck Test showed that sex-appropriate drawings occur at age four and are not more frequent in subsequent years. The Franck Test is easy to administer and, once the scoring techniques were mastered, proved to be surprisingly reliable for so complex a procedure. In a discussion of the Franck Test, Meadows makes the point that "What is needed is . . . evidence that certain deviant groups like homoerotics are significantly placed on the scale" (1959:234). The present report attempts to fill this omission in the literature by linking the Franck Test to errors in sex-role behavior.

Gough's Brief Femininity Scale (Gough, 1952) is a true-false test composed of attitude and interest items, such as "I like mechanics magazines," which measures secondary, conscious sex identity. The 58-item form, most widely used in the studies sponsored by Whiting, was used. This "Gough Test" was chosen because it was meant for adolescents and adults, was easy to administer and short enough for our use, posed no scoring problems (*true* or *false* being circled by the subjects and easily scored; the higher the score, the more feminine the subject), and had been used successfully in the past (Munroe, 1964). The 58 items were selected from a larger number and are the ones in which a difference between the answers of men and women has been observed. For evidence on the validity of the test, see Gough (1952).

A Modification of the Strong Vocational Interest Blank M-F Scale. For another test of secondary sex identity, we used selected items from the M-F Scale of the Strong Vocational Interest Blank. Since the Gough Test has not been *widely* used in the 58-item form, a test whose validity was more established had some appeal. However, the entire Strong Vocational Interest Blank was too long to administer, so only those items that were scored on the M-F Scale on the first three sections of the test were selected (later sections of the test were judged too advanced for these subjects). We composed a test of around 100 items.*

According to the scoring manual, the M-F Scale of the Strong Vocational Interest Blank "measures differences in interest of the two sexes." It is therefore useful to us as a measure of secondary sex identity. A detailed

---

* By special permission from the Strong Vocational Interest Blank for Men by Edward K. Strong, Jr. Copyright 1945 by the Board of Trustees of Leland Stanford Junior University.

analysis of the reliability, repeatability, and validity of the Strong Vocational Interest Blank M-F Scale is given in Strong (1943), Chapter 2. Our modification of the Strong Vocational Interest Blank M-F Scale (hereinafter referred to as M-SVIB) consisted of lists of occupations, school subjects, and activities, to which the subject was asked to indicate his response by checking *Like, Indifferent,* or *Dislike.* Items are given weighted scores depending upon the degree of strength of the sex difference measured when the test was constructed. Negative scores are feminine, positive masculine.

A number of items on both the Gough Test and the M-SVIB seemed likely to be difficult for young boys. Further, many of the boys had serious reading problems, complicated by the fact that boys in mental hospitals usually cannot go to school. It was necessary that the interviewer read the tests aloud to many of the boys, so it was decided to read the tests aloud to all. This gave them the opportunity to ask about anything they did not understand and have it explained. Random monitoring of the explanations offered by each interviewer did not suggest any noticeable bias, and the content of the tests is so far removed from the point of interest that it is doubtful the explanations could have been biased in any consistent way anyway. No tests were scored until all testing had been completed, and all were scored blinded to other material.

Measure of physique and constitution

As pointed out in Chapter 1, it is possible that biological factors could account for some of the behavioral differences classified in this study. It was, therefore, necessary to control for biological factors so far as possible. This has been done, to the degree that one is willing to assume that biochemical factors are related to the variable of lean body mass. Kagan and Moss have said:

Let us assume that a boy with low muscle mass is predisposed to initially adopt a passive orientation to the environment. It would be reasonable to argue that the child's future encounters with the social environment might exaggerate these initial tendencies. (1962:82)

Muscle mass, or more accurately, lean body mass, appears genetic in origin (Behnke, 1959). "It is . . . [therefore] reasonable to assume that boys with low muscle mass might have more difficulty perfecting those masculine skills that lead to peer acceptance" (Kagan and Moss, 1962:82). If this difficulty were compounded by the incorporation of our culture's attitude toward males who are small and weak, it might easily insure passivity. Learning experiences might strengthen an initial, unlearned disposition toward passivity *which might have nothing to do with sex-role learning.* Thus it was necessary to control for proportion of lean body mass in our study.

There are several measures of lean body mass that could have been used. The most sophisticated is no doubt potassium-40 counting (Forbes, 1965). Lean body mass (LBM) is calculated by dividing the total body potassium by 68.1 (a value for the potassium content of the LBM as determined by cadaver analysis). Total body potassium is measured in the "whole body scintillation counter," which measures the amount of the naturally occurring radioisotope potassium-40. The procedure enables a fairly exact computation of the relative lean body mass of the subject, as potassium-40 is not found in fat tissue. However, since no whole body scintillation counter was available in the area of the study, and they are not easily portable, another procedure was required.

Two prime substitutes are "the skin fold test" and hand dynamometer scores (Forbes, personal communication). In the skin fold test the triceps is gripped with calipers and measured. This measurement yields a good approximation of body fat (Damon, Stoudt, and McFarland, 1966) and therefore would show a negative correlation for lean for a given weight. The skin fold test is well known in the anthropometric literature (see Wolanski,

1967), and Damon (1965) has found it useful. There is a reliability problem with it, however. The measure depends in part on how hard the calipers are squeezed and the exact placement on the skin. Since there would be two fieldworkers (of quite different physique) and since subjects were expected to be squirmy, the skin fold test was rejected in favor of the second alternative, hand dynamometer scores, which are freer of experiment bias and were more likely to be tolerated by the subjects.

Forbes has found that grip strength, with height controlled, is a good approximation of lean body mass (personal communication). A hand dynamometer is an instrument for measuring grip strength. The subject squeezes the dynamometer as hard as he can, and his maximum score is retained on the instrument so that it can be read by the fieldworker. We tested the grip strength of both hands, and the highest score obtained was used.

Hand dynamometer scores provide a good index of lean body mass. But it was necessary, in addition, to ascertain what *proportion* of the body was lean body mass. Boys with bigger bodies will have higher dynamometer scores, but who is stronger proportionately? Weight is not a good index of size, since it is also responsive to fat. Height is the best control (Forbes, 1964). Since height and size are also related to age our final score of proportion of lean body mass should be unrelated to height or age. Height and hand dynamometer scores are linearly related; the score is Dynamometer (pounds)/Height (inches) −C.* The advantages in terms of reliability of this measure over the skin fold test are obvious, in that the score depends only upon the strength of the

---

* Controlling dynamometer just for height in inches did not achieve independence from age. The resulting scores were significantly related to age (.36). Since age and height are linearly related (Wolanski, 1967), it was obvious that height in inches was not having a strong enough effect. Dynamometer uncontrolled for height was associated .40 with age. In order to accentuate the control of height, a constant (C) was

subject. The advantage of all of these methods of measuring body constitution over more traditional anthropometric judgments of total body style (endomorphy, ectomorphy, and mesomorphy; see Sheldon, 1949) is also obvious. Besides, photographs of individuals were not permitted by the agencies involved, and we needed a method which would be highly reliable yet require contact with the child by only one fieldworker. (Among dynamometers, the Smedley's hand dynamometer is recommended to physical anthropologists considering using this technique. Its dial is the largest and easiest to read, and it is generally more sturdy and reliable than other, for example Collins type, dynamometers.)

One disadvantage to the use of the dynamometer should be mentioned, however. Temperament may exert an influence on scores. An aggressive, rebellious boy may be more likely to try to impress the interviewer with his strength, while a withdrawn subject may be less likely to squeeze hard. In other words, the grip strength test may be a way to assert one's masculinity or avoid it. (For a study relating psychological factors to strength, see Hettinger, 1961.) All subjects were, therefore, repeatedly urged to squeeze as hard as possible, and the interviewer was not satisfied until some redness of the face appeared and considerable exertion was obvious.

Ranking of social class

A standard measure of social class within the United States is Hollingshead's Two Factor Index of Social Position (Hollingshead, 1952), a weighted score of two factors (occupation and education), weighted 7 and 4

---

subtracted from height. The lowest height was 48, so 45 was subtracted from each height, and dynamometer scores were divided by that. This new score of proportion of the body that was lean body mass was not significantly correlated with age ($r = .11$) and was used as our approximation of the proportion of lean body mass.

respectively. The various possible occupations have been listed and ranked as to prestige level. Educational attainment has also been ranked. The rank is multiplied by the weightings, and the two corrected factors yield scores. The families of the boys in the study were asked the occupation of the father (or mother if the father was absent from the household) and his educational level. Then the families were classed 1 to 5 following Hollingshead's guidelines (5 is the lowest social class).

Utilizing the data collected by these methods, we tested the hypotheses presented in Chapter 2. The results are given in Chapter 4.

IV. FINDINGS

The major findings of the study are outlined in this chapter and discussed in Chapter 5. The findings relating to each of the four hypotheses will be considered in turn.

Hypothesis 1

Boys who are labeled "deviant" for exaggeratedly male behavior or for behavior inappropriate to the male role will have greater primary cross-sex identity than boys who are not thus labeled "deviant."

We have determined primary sex identity by the Franck Drawing Completion Test, on which higher scores indicate greater femininity. Boys were grouped according to their behavior, which was classified as exaggeratedly masculine (E), inappropriate to the male role (I), or control (C), as explained in Chapter 3. An analysis of variance testing the significance of the difference among the mean Franck Test scores of the three groups is given in Table 4.1. The results enable us to reject the null hypothesis ($P < .025$), and to conclude that

E and *I* boys have more primary cross-sex identity than the control group. Hypothesis 1 is therefore tentatively confirmed.

One variable which could account for these findings is social class. In Chapter 2 we observed that several studies have shown that aggressiveness is more characteristic of lower-class males than of middle-class males in the United States. Lower-class males should therefore be over-represented in the group of boys who exhibit exaggeratedly male behavior. In addition lower-class males are more likely to come from households where the father is absent. Thus lower-class males should be more likely to have primary cross-sex identity. Therefore it was necessary to determine whether the results in Table 4.1 owed their significance purely to the effect of social class.

Table 4.2 examines the relationship between social class as measured by the Two Factor Index of Hollingshead and the groups based on sex-role behavior. It shows that while *E* boys have a lower mean social class (the higher the score, the lower the social class) than controls, the *I* boys have an even lower one. However, the differences are not statistically significant. Table 4.2

Table 4.1

**Analysis of Variance of Franck Test Scores
for Groups E, I, and C**

Group	N	Mean	Standard Deviation
E	40	18.39	3.19
I	40	18.31	3.01
C	21	16.33	1.24
	101		

$F = 4.2397$;   d.f. $= 2$, 91; $.01 < P < .025$.
(In all tables one-tailed tests are given whenever direction is indicated in the hypothesis.)

Table 4.2

**Analysis of Variance of Social Class
for Groups E, I, and C**

Group	N	Mean	Standard Deviation
E	45	4.02	.94
I	42	4.19	.96
C	25	3.80	1.00
	<u>112</u>		

F = 1.29 with 2, 109 d.f. N.S.

should not be interpreted as saying that lower-class boys in general are more withdrawn than middle-class boys or even that we have failed to replicate the findings of Fannin and Clinard (1965). Our study population is *not* representative of the general population; it is rather a population labeled "deviant." Withdrawn males may stand out in the relatively more aggressive lower-class culture and therefore be more often labeled "deviant." In addition, the cohort as a whole seems weighted toward the lower end of the class ratings.

Social class may have a direct effect on sex identity. Since lower-class males often come from father-absent households, they may more often exhibit primary cross-sex identity. There is a slight tendency at the .05 level of significance for lower-class males to have feminine Franck Test scores (r = .187, N = 100).

While the relationship between social class and cross-sex identity is small, it is possible that the variance attributable to social class may affect our findings about the Franck Test. To test this, an analysis of covariance was performed in which we sought to discover if differences in mean Franck Test scores for the three groups were maintained when the groups were made comparable with respect to social class (McNemar, 1962:366). Table

4.3 gives the results. Franck Test scores are still statistically significantly different. Hypothesis 1 appears to
be upheld, even with the effect of social class held constant. From the Pearson's r within groups we note that
the relationship between Franck Test scores and social
class is largely due to the strength of that relationship
within the I group.

Another variable that could affect the classification of
boys as E, I, or C is proportion of lean body mass. We
chose to measure this variable by dynamometer scores
controlled for height. Table 4.4 shows that the highest
proportion of lean body mass is found in the E boys,
while I boys have the lowest ($P < .01$). This finding
agrees with other findings that lean body mass is associated with overactivity. This in turn serves to corrob-
orate Forbes' work that a dynamometer score controlled
for height is a good approximation of lean body mass,
since we have found it a good predictor of a group in
which overactivity is common, a relationship previously
reported for muscle mass.

Since proportion of lean body mass is associated with
the behaviors we are trying to predict, we must assess

Table 4.3

**Analysis of Covariance of Franck Test Scores for
Groups E, I, and C, Controlling for Social Class**

Group	N	Mean Social Class	Mean Franck Test Score	Pearson's r Between Franck and Social Class
E	37	4.05	18.39	.12
I	37	4.16	18.31	.29
C	21	3.90	16.33	−.10
	95			

Testing differences in Franck Test scores controlling for social
class, $F = 3.654$ with 2, 91 d.f., $P < .05$.

Table 4.4

**Analysis of Variance of Proportion of
Lean Body Mass for Groups E, I, and C**

Group	N	Mean	Standard Deviation
E	39	1.83	.38
I	39	1.53	.42
C	19	1.62	.34
	97		

F = 6.201 with 2, 94 d.f., P < .01

the association of lean body mass with sex identity in order to be sure that the results in Table 4.1 are not due to *this* variable. The scores for proportion of lean body mass correlate with the Franck Test − .07. Lean body mass is not a good predictor of primary cross-sex identity. This is as it should be if lean body mass is genetic in origin and primary sex identity is formed by culture. However, in order to be sure that the small variance shared by proportion of lean body mass and Franck Test scores will not throw Table 4.1 into non-significant areas of agreement, an analysis of covariance was performed so that we could examine the usefulness of primary sex identity in predicting group behavior when the groups were made comparable with respect to proportion of lean body mass. The results, given in Table 4.5, show the Franck Test means still significantly different for the groups (at the .025 level of significance), even with the effect of body constitution statistically controlled. Thus we are confident that the usefulness of primary sex identity in predicting behavior is statistically significant even when the effect of body composition is removed.

To sum up the findings relative to Hypothesis 1, primary cross-sex identity is higher both in the groups

Table 4.5

**Analysis of Covariance of Franck Test Scores for
Groups E, I, and C Controlling for Proportion of
Lean Body Mass (LBM)**

Group	N	Mean LBM	Mean Franck Test Score	Pearson's r Between LBM and Franck
E	39	1.83	18.48	−.24 N.S.
I	39	1.53	18.32	−.00
C	18	1.64	16.22	.06
	96			

Testing differences in Franck Test scores controlling
for lean body mass, $F = 4.437$ with 2, 92 d.f., $P < .025$.

with exaggeratedly male behavior and in the groups
with inappropriate sex-role behavior, and the difference
is maintained even when social class and proportion
of lean body mass are statistically controlled.

Hypothesis 2

Boys labeled "deviant" for inappropriate sex-role behavior will have greater secondary cross-sex identity
than either the boys labeled "exaggeratedly male" or the
boys not labeled "deviant" in terms of their sex-role behavior (controls).

We have two measures of secondary sex identity
available to us: the Gough Test and a modification of the
Strong Vocational Interest Blank M-F Scale (M-SVIB).
Analyses of variance to test whether the means of the
three groups of boys (E, I, and C) were different on
these tests were performed, and the results are given in
Tables 4.6 and 4.7. Table 4.6 shows the I boys to have

Table 4.6

**Analysis of Variance of Gough Test Scores for
Groups E, I, and C
(Higher scores are more feminine)**

Group	N	Mean	Standard Deviation
E	39	23.54	5.16
I	40	28.78	5.81
C	21	23.29	3.23
	100		

$F = 13.0267$ with 2, 97 d.f., $P < .001$.

significantly higher (more feminine) Gough scores ($P < .001$). The null is rejected and Hypothesis 2 is supported. Table 4.7 shows the *I* group with a significantly lower (more feminine) mean on the M-SVIB ($P < .01$). The null hypothesis is again rejected and our hypothesis confirmed.

The similarity of the results reassures us that the tests are tapping the same dimension. Another confirmation

Table 4.7

**Analysis of Variance of Modified Strong Vocational
Interest Blank Test M-F Scale for Groups E, I, and C
(Lower scores are more feminine)**

Group	N	Mean	Standard Deviation
E	39	31.28	33.64
I	40	0.83	40.15
C	21	9.43	45.01
	100		

$F = 6.2964$ with 2, 97 d.f., $.001 < P < .005$.

of this is that the Gough and M-SVIB scores correlate
−.41. The only observable difference in the results is
that on the M-SVIB the controls are lower (more feminine) than the E boys, while there are no differences
on the Gough Test. The question is left open then
whether the E boys have excessively male secondary
sex identity or a normal amount, with their behavior
a function of primary sex identity. In the opinion of the
author these results indicate that the Gough Test is better at measuring femininity, while the M-SVIB is better
at measuring masculinity.

Although social class did not account for behavior
differences (Table 4.2), there was a possibility that it
could have accounted for differences in *secondary* sex
identity, with lower-class boys having more male
secondary sex identity. A Pearson's correlation was
computed for social class and the Gough Test and the
M-SVIB. Social class correlated .10 with the Gough
Test (94 d.f.) and −.05 with the M-SVIB (94 d.f.). Social
class is therefore independent of secondary sex identity
as measured here, since these differences are not significant enough to enable us to reject the null hypothesis. It is possible, however, that if this variance
were extracted from the relationships reported in
Tables 4.6 and 4.7 the level of significance would be
diminished. Therefore analyses of covariance were performed which would test the differences in mean M-
SVIB and Gough Test scores between the E, I, and C
groups when the groups were made comparable with respect to social class. The results are given in Tables
4.8 and 4.9. They show the significance of the differences in Gough Test means enhanced and the M-SVIB
differences maintained. Thus we are confident that
Hypothesis 2 is supported, independent of any contam-
ination by social class.

In Table 4.4 proportion of lean body mass is an effective predictor of behavior. However, this relationship
did not affect the usefulness of primary cross-sex identity

Table 4.8

Analysis of Covariance of Gough Test Scores for Groups E, I, and C, Controlling for Social Class

Group	N	Mean Social Class	Mean Gough Test Score	Pearson's r Between Gough and Social Class
E	36	4.05	23.42	−.06
I	37	4.16	29.03	.13
C	21	3.81	23.29	.20 N.S.
	94			

Testing differences in Gough Test scores controlling for social class, F = 13.42 with 2, 90 d.f., P < .001.

Table 4.9

Analysis of Covariance of Modified Strong Vocational Interest Blank M-F Scale for Groups E, I, and C, Controlling for Social Class

Group	N	Mean Social Class	Mean M-SVIB Score	Pearson's r Between M-SVIB and Social Class
E	36	4.05	32.47	−.26 N.S.
I	37	4.16	1.24	.17
C	21	3.81	9.43	−.14
	94			

Testing differences in M-SVIB scores controlling for social class, F = 5.75 with 2, 90 d.f., P < .005.

in accounting for both types of errors in sex-role behavior. Given the association with behavior, it is possible
that proportion of lean body mass exerts an effect on
secondary sex identity. It was therefore necessary to
examine the relationship of proportion of lean body mass
to our measures of secondary sex identity. If both E
and I boys have primary cross-sex identity, perhaps high
muscle mass boys *react* to it and become exaggeratedly
masculine, whereas low muscle mass boys might *withdraw* into inappropriate sex-role behavior. The difference in lean body mass may be sufficient to differentiate
between the groups.

Lean body mass is not associated with the Gough Test
($r = -.07$, 96 d.f.), but it is significantly related to the
M-SVIB ($r = .205$, 93 d.f., $P = .05$, two tailed). The association is in the same direction on both tests. There
seems to be some association between proportion of lean
body mass and secondary male sex identity. Therefore
we must ask whether Hypothesis 2 will still be supported
if the effect of proportion of lean body mass is removed.

Tables 4.10 and 4.11 provide an answer. The effective-

Table 4.10

**Analysis of Covariance of Gough Test Scores for
Groups E, I, and C, Controlling for Proportion of
Lean Body Mass (LBM)**

Group	N	Mean LBM	Mean Gough Test Score	Pearson's r Between LBM and Gough
E	38	1.85	23.42	.06
I	39	1.53	28.79	.02
C	18	1.63	24.0	−.21 (N.S.)
	95			

Testing differences in Gough Test scores controlling for proportion of lean body mass, $F = 11.26$ with 2, 91 d.f., $P < .01$.

Table 4.11

Analysis of Covariance of Modified Strong Vocational Interest Blank M-F Scale for Groups E, I, and C, Controlling for Proportion of Lean Body Mass (LBM)

Group	N	Mean LBM	Mean M-SVIB Score	Pearson's r Between LBM and M-SVIB
E	38	1.85	32.26	.30
I	39	1.53	.03	.06
C	18	1.63	8.22	−.18
	95			.21

Testing differences in M-SVIB scores controlling for proportion of lean body mass, $F = 4.88$ with 2, 91 d.f., $P < .025$.

ness of the Gough Test in predicting group behavior is maintained, as is the usefulness of the M-SVIB. It is interesting to note that there is a relationship between the M-SVIB and proportion of lean body mass only for the E group, with neither of the other groups showing a significant Pearson's r between proportion of lean body mass and M-SVIB. This suggests that while a high proportion of lean body mass may make a boy even more exaggeratedly male than he might have been anyway, it is not a crucial factor in determining secondary male identity.

Hypothesis 3

The families of boys with behavior inappropriate to the male role will be marked by father absence. Boys with exaggeratedly male behavior will have experienced father absence in early childhood, followed by some male influence in later childhood.

Table 4.12

Father Absence for Groups E, I, and C

	Total	*E*	*I*	*C*
Father absent throughout child's life	8	6	0	2
Father absent in first four years, then present rest of time	14	7	6	1
Father present in first four years, then absent sometime up to present	42	15	18	9
Father present throughout child's life	54	20	21	13
	118	48	45	25

Table 4.12 shows the extent of father absence in the three groups. It is plain that *I* boys are underrepresented (indeed absent) in the one cell in which they should have been present according to our hypothesis. The rest of the table is remarkably close to a chance distribution. Hypothesis 3 therefore fails.

Hypothesis 4

Boys with exaggeratedly male behavior will share more household tasks with their fathers, and boys with inappropriate sex-role behavior will share more household tasks with their mothers.

Taking the score for overlap of tasks from the sheet concerning division of labor in the household (negative scores indicate more overlap with father, positive with mother), we tested Hypothesis 4. Table 4.13 shows the results for the three groups. As predicted, *I* boys more often share tasks with mothers. The results parallel our earlier finding in connection with Hypothesis 2 relating *I* behaviors to secondary sex identity. Thus we gain new

Table 4.13

Analysis of Variance of Number of Tasks Shared with Parents (Negative Scores Indicate More Overlap with Father, Positive Scores More Overlap with Mother)

Group	N	Mean	Standard Deviation
E	29	−0.1034	1.2913
I	30	1.0667	1.6595
C	14	−0.7143	0.6112
	73		

$F = 9.7589$ with 2, 70 d.f., $P < .001$.

confidence, not only in our measures of secondary sex identity, but also in the index of division of labor used. That the controls more often shared tasks with the father than did the E boys would seem to be related to the studied independence and rebelliousness of the latter. The index of division of labor is independent of Franck Test scores ($r = -.12$) and M-SVIB scores ($r = -.13$) and slightly correlated with Gough Test scores ($r = .24$).

Factor Analysis of Behaviors

As the boys in our cohort were coded, many different behaviors were included under each of the three categories, E, I, and C. It is necessary now to ask whether the different behaviors are all equally related to sex identity or some are more related than others, indicating that our labels should be more specific. In order to determine whether one of the behaviors classed E, for example, was so crucial that it made it appear that the entire E group supports our hypotheses, a factor analysis of the behaviors was carried out in the following way.

Summary cards had been made for each boy by each coder preparatory to the coding reported in Chapter 3.

That coding, of known reliability, was used in the analysis already reported in this paper. Afterwards, all individual behavior descriptions were recorded on cards. There were about two hundred recognizably distinct behaviors reported for the entire cohort. These were arranged into what ultimately became 18 categories, 7 of which were exaggeratedly masculine (*E*), 5 of which were inappropriate to the male role (*I*), and 5 of which were control based on the outlines of the sex roles discussed in Chapter 1. One, *drinking*, could not be classed. Note that behaviors were being classified this time, rather than boys as had been done previously. (By coding each boy's behaviors, these categories could have been used to reclassify the boys. Individual behaviors they exhibited could have been scored—for example, 4 *E*, 2 *I*, and 2 *C* behaviors reported—thus making more precise our notion about which behaviors were dominant. However, this method would have overlooked differences in severity of individual behaviors, so the previous coding of the boys was utilized.)

The 18 Behavior Clusters are listed below, with summaries of the behaviors included in each. The number following each description refers to the number of boys exhibiting each behavior.

Exaggeratedly male (E) behaviors:

1. *Aggressive to things:* destructive, steals, commits arson. (54 boys)

2. *Physically aggressive to people:* violent, bullying, homicidal, sadistic, revengeful. (64 boys)

3. *Verbally aggressive:* loud, swearing, sassy, argumentative, belligerent, hostile, mean, teasing. (58 boys)

4. *Defiant:* defies authority, rebellious, won't conform, wants own way, won't take "no" for an answer, lacks guilt, won't study, is disobedient, runs away, is truant, stubborn, and strong willed, sociopathic. (61 boys)

5. *Trouble-making:* active, getting attention, making commotion. (30 boys)

6. *Sex acting-out (male):* sexual relations with opposite sex, rape, sex play, exaggerated sex behavior. (11 boys)

7. *Behavior normal to the male role but inappropriate to the situation or the boys' age:* independent, having delusions of grandeur, boastful, ambitious, gregarious, demanding. (25 boys)

Behaviors inappropriate to the male sex role (I):

8. *Sexual acts (not male):* exhibitionism, fellatio, masturbation, passive homosexual acts. (11 boys)

9. *Emotional:* crying, nervous, moody, sensitive, artistic, anxious. (39 boys)

10. *Sissy:* more friendly with girls than boys, won't work. (4 boys)

11. *Finicky:* too neat, bothered by noise, psychosomatic complaints, irritable. (12 boys)

12. *Withdrawn:* introverted, quiet, passive, shy, keeps to self, stays home. (66 boys)

Control (C) behaviors:

13. *Immature:* babyish, temperamental, messy, has tantrums, sucks thumb, wets bed. (53 boys)

14. *School problems:* lazy, slow, underachiever, school failure, goof off. (42 boys)

15. *Physical disease:* epilepsy, brain damage, cerebral palsy, speech defect, retardation. (Note that in the coding that was used earlier if any of these was present the case was usually a control.) (14 boys)

16. *Self-destructive:* threatens suicide, "he wants to die," attempts suicide. (15 boys)

17. *Intrapsychic distress:* depressed, morbid, confused, schizophrenic, paranoid, has breakdown, hallucinations, phobias, insomnia, leveled affect, feels helpless, has low opinion of self, feels rejected. (47 boys)

18. *Drinking:* use of alcohol or drugs, alcoholic. (12 boys)

Note that while many boys were described as having
C behaviors, relatively few of the boys themselves were
coded as belonging to the control group (see Chapter 3).
This suggests that the control behaviors were accompanied by errors in sex-role behavior which overshad-
owed them in the judgment of the coders. It may also
suggest that the more exotic errors in sex-role behavior
were likely to be weighted more heavily than the more
mundane control behaviors. It may be that we have coded
more boys as E or I than we might have, which may account for the relative paucity of controls shown in Table
3.2.

Table 4.14 presents mean Franck Test, Gough Test,
and M-SVIB scores for each cluster. Since there are so
few control behaviors without accompanying errors in
sex-role behavior, individual comparison among the behavior clusters in terms of the Franck Test are difficult.
Most of the boys in the study should have high Franck
Test scores since the E and I boys predominate. It is
difficult to pull enough of the high Franck Test scores
over to one side to significantly change the averages for
those lacking the behavior. This presumably accounts
for the lack of variation in the Franck Tests' means in
Table 4.14. Differences in Gough Test and M-SVIB scores
are obtainable. The control means from Chapter 3 are
given for comparison.

*Table 4.14 suggests that certain behaviors included
under the labels* E *and* I *are predicted better by our
theory than are others.* Behavior Cluster 4, *defiant,* is
the prototype behavior of the E group in terms of its
relationship to primary cross-sex and secondary male
identity. Similarly, Cluster 12, *withdrawn,* is the prototype behavior of the I boys with both primary and secondary cross-sex identity. Cluster 9, *emotional,* is also
close to the ideal pattern for I boys. The numbers of
defiant and *withdrawn* boys are so large that *they alone
could account for the variability between the* E *and* I
groups. In one of the E clusters, Cluster 5, the Franck

Test mean for the troublemakers is only slightly higher than that for the controls. Sissies (Cluster 10) also unexpectedly have high M-SVIB scores, but the numbers here are very small. In any event, Table 14.4 suggests that the results presented earlier should be qualified.

Table 4.14

Mean Scores on the Franck Test, Gough Test, and M-SVIB for All Boys Exhibiting Behaviors in Each of 18 Behavior Clusters

		Number Tested	Franck Test (higher score = more feminine primary sex identity)	Gough Test (higher score = more feminine secondary sex identity)	M-SVIB (lower score = more feminine secondary sex identity)
Behavior Clusters					
E:	1. Aggressive to things	43	17.63	25.15	18.68
	2. Physically aggressive to people	51	17.62	24.94	16.80
	3. Verbally aggressive	50	18.10	24.49	24.59
	4. Defiant	51	18.66	23.84	30.72
	5. Trouble-making	27	16.47	25.00	19.31
	6. Sex acting-out (male)	8	17.88	24.38	15.38
	7. Normal but inappropriate male behavior	20	18.13	25.40	19.65
I:	8. Sexual acts (not male)	9	17.17	27.78	11.11
	9. Emotional	35	18.14	26.17	3.17
	10. Sissy	4	19.00	25.75	30.25
	11. Finicky	11	18.84	26.10	11.73
	12. Withdrawn	58	18.02	27.26	6.57
C:	13. Immature	47	18.13	26.80	15.80
	14. School problems	37	18.42	24.68	12.16
	15. Physical disease	10	17.80	24.78	3.33
	16. Self-destructive	14	17.45	28.71	−19.64
	17. Intrapsychic distress	40	17.93	26.55	4.29
	18. Drinking	10	17.42	21.60	16.90
Control means from Chapter 3			16.33	23.29	9.43

Instead of talking about E boys, perhaps we should limit ourselves to *defiant* boys; instead of speaking of I boys, perhaps we should speak of *withdrawn* or *emotional* boys. As far as the control behaviors are concerned, Clusters 13, *immature,* and 14, *school problems,* seem to have higher primary cross-sex identity than the control group average, while Cluster 16, *self-destructive,* seems high on secondary feminine identity. This last relates perhaps to the findings that women are more likely to threaten suicide or attempt and fail, while men are more likely to actually commit suicide (see Farberow and Shneidman, 1961). The fact that the control behaviors, Clusters 13 to 17, taken together, do not have lower Franck Test scores suggests, as we have previously indicated, that these behaviors are often manifest in boys who also manifest errors in sex-role behavior. When those boys whose C behaviors were accompanied by strong I or E behaviors are removed, as in our previous coding discussed in Chapter 2, boys classed as C furnish the normally low Franck Test scores.

Table 4.14 suggests that Cluster 4, *defiant,* on the one hand, and Clusters 12, *withdrawn,* and 9, *emotional,* on the other, should be substituted for our labels E and I. To test whether this was necessary, a factor analysis (Harman, 1960), which would give an indication of whether these behaviors were indeed isolated in their relationship to sex identity, was performed. Each behavior cluster was scored as follows: $0 =$ absent, $1 =$ present, or $2 =$ strongly present. Table 4.15 presents the correlation matrix upon which the factor analysis was performed. By inspection, we learn that E behaviors are interrelated and negatively related to I behaviors; I behaviors are somewhat interrelated and negatively related to E behaviors, while C behavior clusters appear unrelated to either, except for *drinking,* which correlates well with the E behavior clusters.

In performing the factor analysis, we sought to answer the question, Are only Clusters 4 and 12 associated with

Table 4.15

Initial Correlation Matrix of Behavior Clusters

	1	2	3	4	5	6	7	8	9
1		356	238	491	286	053	042	−028	−157
2			428	364	178	163	−018	−160	−212
3				436	289	131	183	−072	−175
4					166	202	246	025	−294
5						005	230	−024	−036
6							008	060	−172
7								−004	024
8									029

	10	11	12	13	14	15	16	17	18
1	−157	−146	−292	069	−005	071	−091	−121	180
2	−180	−204	−338	068	−145	170	−135	−324	142
3	−161	−243	−322	086	−015	−064	−085	−198	243
4	−057	−193	−423	−038	001	−084	001	−194	308
5	−098	−073	−233	−033	147	019	−140	−148	409
6	−055	−096	−149	038	−063	−044	−108	−120	−095
7	−090	−158	−243	−158	−015	032	−065	−067	−001
8	083	083	088	099	005	−065	−009	141	006
9	064	383	207	−135	−122	−053	067	057	−024
10		612	181	−028	191	−065	−065	−017	−057
11			166	−027	089	−057	−043	−086	−101
12				−030	−188	−168	177	379	−084
13					116	−010	165	−036	−108
14						−135	−108	−264	180
15							−067	−055	−050
16								353	−034
17									−067
18									

Table 4.16

Correlation Coefficients of the 18 Behavior Clusters with the 8 Principal Factors

	Behavior Clusters	Factor 1	Factor 2	Factor 3	Factor 4	Factor 5	Factor 6	Factor 7	Factor 8
E:	1. Aggressive to things	−.59	−.07	.01	.11	.01	.37	.21	.00
	2. Physically aggressive to people	−.65	−.02	−.28	−.01	.12	.41	−.11	−.01
	3. Verbally aggressive	−.65	−.00	.12	.01	−.09	.13	−.20	.10
	4. Defiant	−.70	.03	.15	.21	−.33	.20	−.04	.18
	5. Trouble-making	−.47	.29	.45	−.12	.16	−.03	.18	−.14
	6. Sex acting-out (male)	−.25	−.07	−.38	.18	−.53	−.04	−.12	−.24
	7. Normal but inappropriate male behavior	−.29	.01	.26	−.39	−.41	−.34	.20	.45
I:	8. Sexual acts (not male)	.14	.05	.15	.35	−.41	−.02	.62	−.30
	9. Emotional	.42	.19	.25	−.40	−.04	.30	.00	.14
	10. Sissy	.35	.64	−.08	.18	−.19	.25	.02	.14
	11. Finicky	.45	.66	−.07	−.00	−.11	.40	.05	.16
	12. Withdrawn	.67	−.16	.20	.09	.01	.17	−.17	−.28
C:	13. Immature	−.04	−.09	−.25	.62	.31	−.02	.25	.24
	14. School problems	−.08	.57	.06	.33	.29	−.51	−.01	−.08
	15. Physical disease	−.11	−.12	−.34	−.42	.32	.14	.57	−.00
	16. Self-destructive	.24	−.43	.29	.32	.11	.18	−.03	.51
	17. Intrapsychic distress	.43	−.51	.39	.12	−.11	−.09	.14	−.04
	18. Drinking	−.38	.21	.61	.07	.24	.11	−.07	.31

sex identity, or are they really the endpoints of a behavioral continuum, thus justifying our use of more general labels? The results of the factor analysis are presented in Table 4.16.

The first factor generated, which by definition is the one that accounts for the most variance, is clearly the one called "errors in sex-role behavior" in this report. Here the positive side is I, the negative E, and Factor 1 would have to be labeled "inappropriate to the male role." The factor loadings for Factor 1 almost exactly parallel our coding of E, I, or C above. We are confident that our classification of these behaviors makes sense in terms of sex role. Also, we are somewhat reassured that our previous coding of *E*, *I*, and *C* groups of boys is justified.*

Exciting as these findings are, we can further test whether Clusters 4 and 12 are uniquely associated with sex identity or are endpoints of a continuum of errors in sex-role behavior. Table 4.16 shows that the highest negative factor loading is for Cluster 4. The highest positive factor loading is for Cluster 12. Thus, the behaviors which the tests of sex identity appear to predict best in Table 4.14 are the behaviors most highly correlated with Factor 1, *inappropriate to the male role*. This justifies considering these behaviors as endpoints of one behavioral continuum. Therefore, the further from .00 association with Factor 1 that a cluster is, the more extreme the scores of cognitive sex identity should be. The use of the more general categories *E* and *I* is supported.

Note that *drinking* (Cluster 18) is an *E* characteristic, while *intrapsychic distress* (Cluster 17) appears to be an *I* characteristic. *Drinking* makes intuitive sense as "protest masculinity" within this teen-age group. That *intrapsychic distress* is an *I* characteristic is probably due to two points: (1) Cluster 9, *emotional*, an *I* behavior cluster, includes nervousness. We tried to separate nervousness from other symptoms of intrapsychic distress, but apparently they are too closely interrelated. (2) The inclusion of schizophrenic behavior in Cluster 17 means that a group of withdrawn, passive boys are included in this category. Thus, these categories are not really mutually exclusive. A boy whose behavior was classified under Cluster 17 would most likely show behavior classified under Clusters 12 or 9 as well.

Cluster 8, *sexual acts* (*not male*), is weakly associated with Factor 1, but because of small numbers it need not be moved. Cluster 16 appears to be an *I* char-

---

* We have coded sex-role behaviors as if they were on one continuum (*E*, *C*, *I*) rather than on two (male, not male; female, not female), as Gonen and Lansky (1965) have suggested is necessary.

acteristic, which validates our previous statement that attempts or threats of suicide appear to be a feminine characteristic, cognitively as well as behaviorally.

To pursue the relationship of factor loadings with sex identity itself, the behavior clusters were reordered according to their factor loadings with Factor 1. Table 4.17 gives mean ranks for Franck Test, Gough Test, and M-SVIB scores for the 4 most positive factor loadings (I), the 10 intermediate factor loadings (C), and the 4 most negative factor loadings (E). Gough Test scores decrease as the factor loadings decrease, showing an increasing masculinity as the E end is reached. The M-SVIB scores increase as the factor loadings decrease, again showing increased masculinity as the E end is reached. Franck Test scores are higher at each end of the continuum than they are in the middle, reflecting our theory that both E and I clusters have more feminine primary sex identity than controls. However, the Franck Test scores seem to lose effectiveness on the negative (male) side of the continuum. We shall discuss this in the next chapter.

As a more refined test of these relationships, factor scores were obtained for each boy for each of the first

Table 4.17

Mean Ranks * for Gough Test, M-SVIB, and Franck Test Scores When Behavior Clusters Are Arranged by Factor Loadings for Factor 1

	Gough Test	M-SVIB	Franck Test
4 most positive factor loadings (I)	5.2	14.5	6.5
10 intermediate factor loadings (C)	9.9	9.4	10.7
4 most negative factor loadings (E)	12.8	4.5	9.5

* Obtained by averaging means for each behavior cluster.

Table 4.18

**Pearson Product-Moment Correlation Coefficients
for Factor Scores and Test Scores**

	Franck Test	Gough Test	M-SVIB
Factor 1	.042	.316	−.267
N	101	100	100
Factor 2	.046	−.250	.192
N	101	100	100
Factor 3	−.103	.051	−.054
N	101	100	100
Factor 4	.020	.083	.004
N	101	100	100

four factors.* This score is calculated by multiplying an individual's score on each of the behavior clusters by the factor loadings and summing for all categories. If, as we suspect, behavior is predictable by sex identity, the following relationships between the factor scores for Factor 1 and the tests measuring sex identity should be found:

1. The Franck Test should not be linearly correlated with factor scores since Franck Test scores should be highest for both behavior extremes (*E* and *I*).

2. The Gough Test should be positively related to Factor 1 scores, since the scores increase as amount of *I* behavior increases relative to *E* behavior and Gough Test scores increase with femininity.

3. The scores on the M-SVIB should be negatively related to Factor 1 scores, since M-SVIB scores decrease with femininity.

In fact these expectations are fulfilled (see Table 4.18). Factor 1 scores correlate only .04 with Franck Test

---

* John Whiting suggested this procedure. Factors 5 to 8 were thought to involve too little variance to justify the procedure.

scores, but .32 with Gough Test scores (P < .0025) and −.27 with M-SVIB scores (P < .005). Factor 2 is related in the opposite direction with the Gough Test and M-SVIB, but not so strongly (r = −.25, .19, respectively; P < .05). While the meaning of the factor is uncertain, this suggests that *school problems* are related to strong secondary masculinity, while *intrapsychic distress* is related to secondary femininity. Since *sissy* and *finicky* are positively related to Factor 1 as well, their small numbers would seem to best account for their inconsistency. Factors 3 and 4 are unrelated to any tests.

Taken in the context of the theory and other findings outlined in this report, these findings furnish evidence that sex identity can be used to predict sex-role behavior, but perhaps more importantly they open some avenues for pursuing this problem in the future by validating the notion of errors in sex-role behavior as a viable concept.

V. DISCUSSION OF FINDINGS

We have been a good deal more successful in using sex identity to predict sex-role behavior than we have been in accounting for sex identity itself. This chapter begins with a discussion of this problem, then moves on to discuss our other findings.

Factors Affecting Sex Identity

Father absence

Our failure to discover the relationship between father absence and sex-role behavior anticipated by Hypothesis 3 is probably a function of two factors. First, the validity of our data concerning the household history of each boy is questionable. Subjects have proven to be poor informants in this kind of interviewing (see Chapter 3). They often do not accurately remember when certain events happened. There is also the likelihood of some deliberate distortion. Women are sometimes unwilling to admit separations from their husbands. In one case, we knew from hospital records that a woman had been divorced and remarried twice during the life of the child, but she reported to us that her present husband had been in the house from the birth of the child. It is also to be expected that some will be unwilling to report the presence of common-law husbands or husbands in marriages that did not work out. Thus, some men who were not there will be represented as present in the household and some who were there will not be reported. If such misrepresentations were widespread, these data have very little validity. Since we were unable to replicate the findings of others concerning a link between father absence and sex identity (presented in Chapter 1), this is likely to be the case. We were aware of some of these limitations when the study was planned, and that is why we used direct tests of sex identity in addition to attempting to relate behavior to household histories. Incidentally, father absence did not predict scores on any of the tests either. Were we to believe in our data, it therefore would seem to be unrelated to sex identity as well as behavior!

Secondly, father absence is a rather gross approximation of what really needs to be examined. Other investigators have shown the quality of the father's relationship with the child to be important. Sears found that American boys can be feminized by the father's sexual anxieties or by the severity of the mother's aggression control, and type of punishment (Sears, 1965). In a study not yet published when this study was carried out, Sears, Rau, and Alpert (1966) found a closed, anxious, nonpermissive attitude on the part of either or both parents to be conducive to femininity in children of both sexes, as are the use of very physical punishment and severe control of aggression. They hypothesized that "permissiveness encourages the development of the active, adventurous free-ranging quality of behavior that characterizes the male role, and that punitiveness creates pressure toward the more passive and conforming behavior that typifies the female role" (Sears, Rau, and Alpert, 1966:198).

Sears, Rau, and Alpert (1966) found that, for boys, imitation of the mother is related to a high degree of nurturance and responsiveness on her part. Nurturance and responsiveness on the part of the father do *not* cause imitation in boys. In regard to our findings then, even in a father-absent household, imitation of an unnurturant and unresponsive mother seems unlikely. The process of identification, here linked to nurturance rather than control of resources, is apparently more complex than we have indicated. Each parent's role must be examined separately, and this is presumably true of envied figures as well as nurturant ones. Control of resources by men, for example, cannot any longer be assumed to be equivalent to control by women in its effect on the child, any more than nurturance can.

If we assume for a moment that our data on household history are valid, it is suggested that in the United States father absence is not a good predictor of sex-role behavior. Rather some notion of the importance of the father and the quality of his relationship with the son, following particularly this recent work of Sears, Rau, and Alpert, must be introduced in order to predict differences in sex-role behavior. The mother's role would also have to be examined.

Other intra-familial factors

Intra-familial factors other than parent salience may be operating as well. The effects of siblings and of birth order should be investigated. Rosenberg and Sutton-Smith showed that presence of an older sibling of the opposite sex induces sex-role problems and anxieties (Rosenberg and Sutton-Smith, 1964). Our data do not seem to substantiate this. The *I* boys are described as having, not more older sisters, but more older brothers than the other boys.

All the *I* boys had fathers who were present, which seems to support Greenstein (1966). Thus with more

Table 5.1

Presence of Older Siblings for the Three Groups of Boys

	Older Brothers	Older Sisters	No Older Siblings
E	12	16	22
I	18	11	18
C	7	7	12

Testing that *I* boys more often have older brothers than all others, $X^2 = 2.44$, d.f. = 1, $.20 < P < .10$.

older brothers and with fathers present in all cases there is a suggestion that there are more older males in the households of *I* boys. One way of explaining why their behavior is inappropriate to the male role might be the following: The family has a component of male roles which must be filled, and these roles may be expected to be filled by the older male figures in the household. The boy whose behavior is here labeled "inappropriate" to the male role enters, and, figuratively speaking, there is little left for him to do. He may, therefore, try the female role, which is comparatively empty, perhaps to differentiate himself from his older male siblings. Note, however, that while this would explain *imitation* of the female role, it would not explain *identification* with female figures.

Extra-familial factors

It is possible that the lower-class gang is an institutionalized reaction to primary cross-sex identity (Cohen, 1955; Miller, 1958; Rohrer and Edmonson, 1964).

. . . [The gang] springs from the little boy's search for masculinity he cannot find at home becoming at first a protest against femininity and then an assertion of hypervirility. On the way it acquires a structuring in which the aspirations and goals of the matriarchy or the middle class are seen as soft, effeminate, and despicable. The gang ideology of masculine independence is formed from these perceptions and the gang then sees its common enemy not as a class, nor even as a sex, but as the "feminine principle" in society. (Rohrer and Edmonson, 1964:162–163)

The gang may prepare the boys for adult life by insuring secondary male identity in a fashion similar to the separation phase in many *rites de passage*. The peer group then is possibly an important element in formation of secondary sex identity. Miller reported:

As the boys approached the age of twenty, they were subject to a variety of pressures to leave the physical, psychic, and social status of adolescence and assume the status of young adult. . . . The boy's corner gang and its particular way of life was defined, both by adults and the boys themselves, as appropriate to adolescence but inappropriate to adulthood. . . . The corner group served to provide its members a mechanism of restriction and limitation as well as a climate of nurturance. With the weakening of the solidarity of the gang in prospect, its members were induced to seek out new environments which provided similar elements of nurturance and control. While these elements could be and were found in the armed forces, correctional institutions, and factories, the device most generally available and most frequently utilized was marriage. (Miller, 1964:48)

Partial support for the notion that gangs affect secondary sex identity comes from the fact that of the six *E* boys in our study whose fathers were never present, five were from the lowest social class, and one was from the next lowest. Since these boys with predominantly *E* behavior came from the social strata where gangs are most frequent and since their fathers were absent, it could at least be suggested that gang membership influenced their secondary male identity.

But our data offer no real help in determining how sex identification takes place, other than to suggest that it must be necessary to consider a wider range of alternatives than has been considered in the past. In view of the foregoing, as we look back on our initial Hypothesis 3 we recognize it as an example of the kind of naiveté which is likely to cause problems when an anthropologist or any social scientist goes outside his major area of competence. Thus the etiology of sex identification remains a problem of prime importance, particularly since we have been successful in demonstrating that sex identity is useful in predicting adolescent errors in sex-role behavior. We now move on to discuss those findings.

Primary Cross-Sex Identity and Sex-Role Behavior

Having discussed the findings relating to Hypothesis 3, we now return to those relating to Hypothesis 1: Boys who are labeled "deviant" for exaggeratedly male behavior or for behavior inappropriate to the male role will have greater primary cross-sex identity than boys who are not thus labeled "deviant."

The E and I groups were found to have significantly higher Franck Test scores, indicating more primary cross-sex identity, than the controls, even when the groups were made comparable with respect to social class and proportion of lean body mass. Table 4.1 shows that the standard deviations for the E and I groups are twice the standard deviation for the control group. In order to assess the meaning of this, the Franck Test scores were arrayed and trichotomized as presented in Table 5.2. This table shows that the controls have no scores higher than 18 or lower than 14. Hopefully the explanation of the first finding is that our theory is correct, and that Franck Test scores above 18 are good predictors of errors in sex-role behavior.

Table 5.2

Franck Test Scores for Groups E, I, and C

	Franck Test Scores		
Group	10–13	14–18	19–24
E	2	19	19
I	3	19	18
C	0	21	0

However, a Franck Test score of less than 14 also predicts some errors in sex-role behavior, and this is true of both the *E* and *I* groups. This finding appears to be quite contrary to our hypothesis: however, the differences are not great enough to reach significance, and we suspect that the five cases represent inability of the Franck Test to consistently measure what we call primary sex identity, or some failure in coding. The possibility remains, however, that excessively male *primary* sex identity may also predict errors in sex-role behavior. In Chapter 1, over-differentiation of sex roles was said to be deviant because there are occasions when the dominant skills of the other sex are necessary. Intuitively, it makes sense that *E* behaviors could result from too much masculinity as well as from protest against underlying femininity. The *I* boys with very low Franck Test scores, are, however, anomalies. We do not simply dismiss this finding here as a chance association because some *I* boys appear to have more men in their households than either the *E* or *C* groups. This would fit with a low Franck Test score, suggesting that in addition to our main type of *I* boy, with both primary and secondary cross-sex identity, there may also be some *I* boys with primary male and secondary cross-sex identity, whose presence we had not predicted. Note that secondary sex identity still predicts behavior. But this raises the question, How important is primary sex identity to behavior? The main thrust of our findings is that it is important only when considered in the light of secondary sex identity.

We have shown that Franck Test scores, and therefore primary cross-sex identity, are useful predictors of errors in sex-role behavior in boys. Both the E and I boys have higher proportions of primary feminine identity than the controls, and while these differences are not as great as they might be, they do hold up well with the effects of social class and of body constitution removed. Sears, Rau, and Alpert (1966) found for boys "no evidence to support the notion of a cluster of primary identification related behavior. . . ." Our research offers an explanation for their failure. Knowledge of secondary sex identity is necessary to separate exaggeratedly male behavior from inappropriate sex-role behavior for boys. Both begin with primary feminine identity. Knowledge of secondary sex identity is required to predict these disparate behaviors. Therefore it is understandable that to Sears, Rau, and Alpert behavior appeared unpredictable by primary sex identity.

One limitation to the Franck Test findings comes from Tables 4.14 and 4.17. In Table 4.14, Franck Test scores appear to successfully predict only Cluster 4, *defiant*. While we are confident, because of the factor analysis and the means reported for scores on the Gough Test and the M-SVIB in Table 4.17, that this is the end point of a behavioral continuum, the Franck Test mean ranks shown in Table 4.17 are not uniform; they are not equally high on the two tails of the continuum. In fact, inspection of the scores for the other E clusters in Table 4.14 reveals that the Franck Test scores may increase on the E side in Table 4.17 entirely because of the effect of Cluster 4.

This throws into some question the view of *aggression* as "protest masculinity" outlined in Chapter 1. It may be that, not aggression per se, but rather the attitude or mental set which accompanies it, is predicted by primary cross-sex identity. Thus aggression may arise from biochemical factors (see Table 4.4); cultural factors (aggression is more normal and more tolerated in some subcultures); or sociological factors (aggression directed outside the group may increase as group solidarity increases; therefore aggression may be part of social control mechanisms designed to assure conformity within a group). These and a host of other explanations of aggression are available to us (Harrington, n.d.). What our data seem to suggest is that primary cross-sex identity accompanied by conflicting secondary male identity predicts a defiant and rebellious attitude as an error in sex-role behavior. Because such an attitude is often associated with overt aggression, we have been led to believe that aggression per se is explainable in this way.

It must also be remembered that we are dealing with deviant behavior here and therefore our findings cannot suggest that protest masculinity will stand to explain "normal aggression." The attacks of the Dani of New Guinea on their neighbors and the lineman's fury on the football field are culturally sanctioned, learned behaviors which do not obviously require explanations oriented to culturally deviant behavior.* However, those Dani who leap to the fray with reckless abandon and those linemen who dismember the opposing quarterback with defiant relish elicit some suspicion that "protest masculinity" may well explain some aspects of their behavior.

Recognizing these limitations may give us a fuller picture than we had before, because we see that aggression springs from many sources, including some nonpathological ones, but that we can explain the defiant, rebellious, guiltless kind of aggression discussed here in terms of "protest masculinity." This may suggest to psychiatrists that explanations of sociopathy relating

---

* Although the dynamics we have described may throw light on these more general patterns.

to conflicts in sex identity may have some utility. Given the relative permanence of primary sex identity generally assumed in the literature, this may suggest an explanation for why these kinds of boys are less amenable to successful treatment than others.

Secondary Sex Identity and Sex-Role Behavior

Our findings in regard to Hypothesis 2 are clear with the exception of one point. We are quite sure that I boys have secondary cross-sex identity. It is not so certain whether the secondary sex identity of E boys is male to an excessive degree or rather to the same degree as that of the controls. The factor analysis suggests the former. But in regard to the sharing of household tasks, we know that E boys have slightly less overlap of tasks with their fathers than the C boys.

We have found cognitive tests of secondary sex identity useful in predicting behavior. I boys have both primary and secondary female identity more often, as predicted. E boys more often have primary female identity and secondary male identity. We have also demonstrated that E boys share tasks with the father around the house, if they share at all, while I boys share tasks with the mother. Errors in sex-role behavior then seem to be errors in sex-role learning, accountable by theories of sex identity. To say that such a theory is useful does not imply that identification is the only way sex-role learning takes place, but there *is* sufficient utility in the theory to justify further research. The ability of our findings to stand up even when the effects of social class and body composition were removed is especially encouraging.

We have found support for Kagan and Moss's theory that proportion of lean body mass can account for passivity. This is not to be accepted as proof of a relationship with inborn factors, however. Developmental factors may have effected the relationship. Damon, Stoudt, and MacFarland state:

... [exercise] can increase strength and endurance within the limits imposed by a person's innate physical potential. Differences in strength as measured before and after training can be considerable. ... Increases in strength after training of as much as 100 per cent ... have been recorded ... increments above ... [30 per cent have been] observed in normal subjects after 2 weeks of training. (1966:203)

It is possible, of course, that the differences in body composition detected by our instrument may have resulted to some extent from greater activity (more exercise) on the part of the E boys; therefore we may have measured, not purely inborn factors, but inborn plus developmental factors. However, if inborn factors accentuated by exercise did not affect the associations with primary and secondary identity, it seems reasonable to assume that biology alone would not, as exercise would only accentuate the differences we were seeking. We cannot prove or disprove Kagan and Moss's suggestion that behavior and inborn factors are related because our study was not designed to do so; we can say that proportion of lean body mass does not account for our sex identity findings. Further, the strength of the finding linking lean body mass with behavior suggests that the physiological etiology of passivity and aggression seems fully worth pursuing in future studies. Not dealt with here is the effect of body type upon others' expectations of the individual, and upon their willingness to label him as "deviant." To give two examples: a heavily muscled mesomorph may be expected to be aggressive and loud, and therefore may be given more leeway in those behaviors than an ectomorph in whom such behaviors might be thought bizarre; a mesomorph with feminine or sissy behavior might be labeled "deviant" before an ectomorph with the same behaviors who has more leeway in this regard thanks to cultural stereotypes.

A Note on Treatment

It was noted earlier that conditions associated with errors in sex-role behavior have been found to be intransigent to treatment. Primary cross-sex identity is presumably important because of its effect on imitation, but beyond this it is difficult to assess its significance. Our findings support our reasoning that primary cross-sex identity may either be expressed (*I* behaviors) or reacted to (*E* behaviors). Yet because this study was done on a deviant population, it is unclear whether it is possible to lead a "normal" life given primary cross-sex identity. Further the ability of sex identity to predict errors in sex-role behavior is not sufficient evidence to conclude that it exists inside these boys' heads. Therefore, it is not reasonable to assume that treatment programs for such boys should seek to "cure" or prevent primary cross-sex identity by manipulating the social environment as Whiting, Kluckhohn, and Anthony (1958) suggest. This study establishes a link between measures of primary and secondary sex identity, on the one hand, and behavior, on the other. Yet there are a number of *E* and *I* boys who do not have primary cross-sex identity as measured by the Franck Test but behave as if they did. There are probably other explanations for their behavior than ours, and we should not claim that our theory is the only way to account for it. That we were able to predict behavior using primary identification theory does not, of course, mean that this is the only way that errors in sex-role learning occur. There are other types of learning theories that may account equally well for the same percentages of variance. Nor does the success of our prediction demonstrate that the cross-sex identity assumed to exist in the head of a boy who scored high on the various tests is what accounts for his behavior. He may happen to have cross-sex identity, but his behavior might be attributable to another kind of learning, or failure to learn, or to immediate social or cultural factors. What we have shown is that for the group studied errors in sex-role behavior are predictable by psychological theories of identification. In light of the difficulty of predicting such standard diagnostic categories as "sociopath" and "schizophrenic," our results suggest that there is great promise in recent attempts of anthropologists and sociologists to create new categories for those now called "mentally ill" that would reflect normal social roles. (See Harrington and Wilkins, 1966; Scheff, 1966.) For now, they probably could also safely be taken to suggest that it should help to focus some treatment programs for these boys on efforts to increase their knowledge of the appropriate sex role. Boys with exaggeratedly male behavior should be helped to control their masculinity; boys with inappropriate sex-role behavior should be provided educational and occupational rehabilitation to teach them how to perform as adult males.

Within this framework, it is necessary to comment on one aspect of the treatment of these boys. When *I* boys are hospitalized (they are sometimes labeled "preschizophrenic"), they are usually not allowed to attend school. In the hospitals dealt with in our study, there are no programs of occupational rehabilitation for them. Furthermore, the everyday activities of their hospital "world," the ward, are often directed by women (nurses) or occupationally marginal men (attendants). It is not surprising that Cumming (1963) found a population of adult schizophrenics to have a high incidence of what he calls "occupational inadequacy," which is an inability to perform the core of the male role. Our *I* boys have never learned to perform the male role appropriately. However, it is not likely that they will learn to perform it in the setting provided by the kind of treatment they presently receive! Without socialization to the requirements of the adult male role (through school, occupational training, and association with instrumentally competent male figures), the probability of changing their inappropriate sex-role behavior would seem low. Thus the intransigence of the I behaviors to treatment may not be so much due to their underlying cognitive origins as to the fact that the treatment programs are badly bungling the job they set out to do. In fact, they may be exacerbating these social symptoms of occupational inadequacy rather than improving them. Obviously, to give a definitive answer to this question a study addressed directly to this issue would be required.

Conclusions

We have established:

1. that a large group of boys requesting admission to mental health facilities are labeled "deviant" for problems which can usefully be considered errors in sex-role behavior;

2. that these errors include behavior that is exaggeratedly male and not male enough; *

3. that there is an identifiable link between primary and secondary sex identity and behavior in these adolescent boys;

4. that this link is in conformity with our theory: E boys typically have primary cross-sex identity and sec-

---

* These first two points and informal observation for one year of a group of normal adolescents in the United States suggest that the division of labor in U.S. culture is fixing on the adult-child dimension as an organizing principle and increasingly ignoring differences between males and females, to the point that a strong preference for either the male role or the female role may be in and of itself pathological. As we said in Chapter 1, in a sense the boys here labeled E and I have made such a mistake—the E boys having a strong preference for the male role, the I boys a preference for the female. It is not yet clear what the cultural consequences of this postulated reorganization of roles will be.

ondary male identity, whereas *I* boys typically have both
primary and secondary cross-sex identity;

5. that sex identity is useful in predicting behavior
even when social class and body composition are held
constant;

6. that the *I* boys more often share tasks with their
mothers, the *E* boys with their fathers;

7. that boys who exhibit *E* behaviors have not failed
to learn the male role, but rather their uncontrolled
performance of it seems to compensate for an initially
feminine identity; *I* boys seem to be impaired in both
their learning and performance of the male role.

We have established a link between primary and secondary sex identity and errors in sex-role behavior, in
support of the line of reasoning outlined in Chapter 1.
Studies in psychological anthropology that assume such
a relationship appear to be justified in their assumption.
The findings support the predictive power of the notion
of protest masculinity, particularly for defiant, stub-
bornly rebellious types. Most generally, our data suggest that regardless of what happens to an individual
before age ten to establish primary and secondary sex
identities, these identities are useful predictors of errors in sex-role behavior after age twelve. The next steps
to be taken are cross-cultural studies which would vali-
date our findings by demonstrating that sex identity
affects sex-role learning and thereby sex-role behavior,
regardless of how a particular society defines these roles,
and by replicating our own results on a larger sample.

APPENDIX

APPENDIX

Parent Interview About Child's Behavior

1. Explain study and gain compliance.
   I'd like to talk with you about your son.
   He applied at _____ for help _____. Can you tell me why?
2. Can you tell me something about your son?
   What things would he do that bother you? Anything else?
3. What sort of boy is he? (Probe: active-passive; aggressive–non-aggressive; quiet-loud) Studious? Athletic? How much time does he spend at home? When away, is he with other boys or with girls?
4. What kind of boy was he when younger? (Probe: For example, do you remember what kind of *baby* he was?)
   What was he like when a few years older?
   Was there any time when he seemed to change a lot? (If yes, mark time on household sheet and probe then.)
5. Have others complained about him?
   What kind of complaints have they made? (Probe: family members, relatives, neighbors, school teachers, police, friends, others.)
   Does he ever act this way at home? [Ask only if the complaints are different.]
6. How has your son answered these complaints? (Probe: Has he said anything about them?)
   Has he said that anything he does has bothered him?
7. Does the way your son act remind you of anyone in your family? Of any friends? Why? What behavior and who? (If necessary, ask about problem behavior if this has been omitted, or about personality and behavior in general if only problem behavior has been mentioned.)
8. What is he doing now (if he wasn't committed)? School? Job? Nothing?

9. Now could we take a minute to talk about you and
   your husband? (Father's occupation or mother's if
   father absent; title; duties; place of business.)
   How many years of education did your husband
   have? And you?

Household History

1. We would like to know who has been around your son as he grew up. We would like to know whom he has lived with.

   Could you help us by beginning with when he was born. Was he born in a hospital? If yes, when he came home from the hospital, who was living there at that time? By living, we mean actually living in the house, not visiting. A good rule to keep in mind is one month. If longer than one month, he's living in the house; if shorter, it's just a visit.

2. I'm going to record what you tell me about who was living there on this sheet by drawing a line for those living in the house. (Demonstrate.) [See the following page.]

3. Did they stay in the home?

   A. Probe: Was the child ever out of the house? Maybe we should do that first. Is the child still with those who were in the house when he was born? (Block in child's absences with brackets for later probing.)

   B. Probe: Who was living with the child when he was one year old? Two, etc.? Was he ever not with them, etc.? Did anyone else leave the child, or did anyone else join him? That is, did any brothers or sisters leave home, or were any born? (For foster families follow the child through his travels as well as possible.)

(Continue with sheet, encouraging subject to work with us in filling it out.)

Instructions

1. *Household* is defined by the location of the subject.
2. A line drawn through a square indicates the presence of someone in that household. (The subject is by definition always present.)
3. Letter any unusual breaks and describe on attached blank sheets.
4. Mark to the nearest quarter year.
5. *Institution* refers to a mental hospital, children's home, the army, and the like. Any line drawn in this row requires explanation on attached sheet.
6. *Household* is defined spatially as same house or apartment. If relative next door, for example, note on attached sheet.
7. Dual residences (for example, if the child is in a foster home but spends weekends with his parents) should be recorded (one with pen, the other with pencil) and must be explained in detail on attached sheet.

The History of the Household of the Child

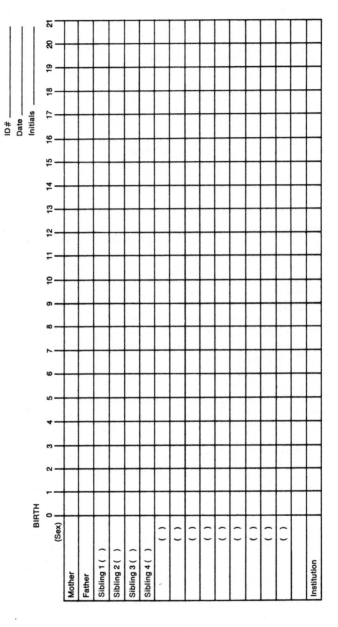

	(Sex)	BIRTH 0	1	2	3	4	5	6	7	8	9	10	11	12	13	14	15	16	17	18	19	20	21
Mother																								
Father																								
Sibling 1 ( )																								
Sibling 2 ( )																								
Sibling 3 ( )																								
Sibling 4 ( )																								
( )																								
( )																								
( )																								
( )																								
( )																								
( )																								
( )																								
( )																								
( )																								
Institution																								

ID # _____
Date _____
Initials _____

95

Division of Labor in the Household

Now I would like to ask you a few questions about who does some of the jobs around your home. Let's start with washing the dishes after supper:

    A. Who does the task?

    B. Does _____ (Name) _____ do this alone?

    C. If no, who helps?

    D. How often?

    E. When someone helps: When you say that

    _____ (Name) _____ helps, do you mean that they do

    it together or does one do it sometimes and the other do it sometimes?

TASKS		FAMILY MEMBERS IN HOUSEHOLD									Non-resident	Relative (specify)	Other (specify)
1) Who washes the dishes after supper?													
2) Who shops for groceries?													
3) Who pays bills, such as telephone and lights?													
4) Who cleans the house (apartment)?													
5) Who moves heavy furniture (cleaning, changing room)?													
6) Who takes care of washing and hanging out clothes?													
7) Who fixes things like clogged drains or electric plugs?													
8) Who gets the children ready for bed?													
9) Who does things like mowing the lawn, cleaning the yard, and cleaning the basement?													
10) Who washes and cleans the car?													
11) Who cooks and prepares meals?													

96

REFERENCES

Aberle, David F., and Kaspar D. Naegele
  1952 Middle class fathers' occupational role and attitudes toward children. American Journal of Orthopsychiatry 22:366–378.
Bach, G. R.
  1946 Father fantasies and father typing and father separated children. Child Development 17:63–79.
Bandura, A.
  1962 Social learning through identification. *In* Nebraska symposium on motivation, M. R. Jones, ed. Lincoln, Nebr., University of Nebraska Press.
Bandura, A., Dorothea Ross, and Sheila A. Ross
  1963 A comparative test of the status envy, social power, and secondary reinforcement theories of identificatory learning. Journal of Abnormal and Social Psychology 67:527–534.
Bandura, A., and R. H. Walters
  1959 Adolescent aggression. New York, Ronald Press.

97

1963   Social learning and personality development. New York, Holt, Rinehart & Winston.

Barry, Herbert III, Margaret K. Bacon, and Irvin L. Child
1957   A cross cultural survey of some sex differences in socialization. Journal of Abnormal and Social Psychology 55:327–333.

Behnke, A. R.
1959   The estimation of lean body weight from skeletal measurements. Human Biology 31:295–315.

Beller, E. K., and B. D. Neubauer
1963   Sex differences and symptom patterns of early childhood. Journal of Child Psychiatry 2:417–433.

Bieliauskas, J.
1965   Recent advances in psychology of masculinity and femininity. Journal of Psychology 60:255–263.

Bohannan, Paul
1965   The differing realms of the law. American Anthropologist 67:33–42.

Brown, D. G.
1956   Sex-role preference in young children. Psychological Monographs: General and Applied 70:1–19.

Brown, Roger
1965   Social psychology. New York, Free Press.

Buros, O. K., ed.
1959   Fifth mental measurements yearbook. Highland Park, N. J., Gryphon Press.

Burton, Roger, and John W. M. Whiting
1961   The absent father and cross-sex identity. Merrill-Palmer Quarterly 7:85–95.

Carlsmith, Karolyn Kuckenberg
1963   Effect of father absence on scholastic aptitude. Unpublished Ph.D. dissertation, Harvard University.

Cumming, Elaine
1966   The naming of infants: a study of role differ-

entiation. Paper read at the American Sociological Association meetings, Miami, Florida.
Cumming, John
1963   The inadequacy syndrome. Psychiatric Quarterly 37:723–733.
Cumming, John, and Elaine Cumming
1962   Ego and milieu. New York, Atherton.
Cutter, W. B.
1964   Household structure, behavior, and personality in Barbados. Unpublished senior honors
thesis, Harvard College.
Damon, Albert
1965   Notes on anthropomorphic technique. American Journal of Physical Anthropology
23:305–311.
Damon, Albert, Howard W. Stoudt, and Ross A. McFarland
1966   The human body in equipment design. Cam-
bridge, Mass., Harvard University Press.
D'Andrade, Roy G.
1962   Paternal absence and cross-sex identification.
Unpublished Ph.D. dissertation, Harvard
University.
1966   Sex differences and cultural institutions.
In The development of sex differences, E.
E. Maccoby, ed. Stanford, Calif., Stanford
University Press.
Dawe, H. C.
1934   An analysis of 200 quarrels of preschool
children. Child Development 5:139–156.
Devons, E., and M. Gluckman
1964   Introduction. *In* Closed systems and open
minds, M. Gluckman, ed., Chicago, Aldine.
Durrett, Mary E.
1959   The relationship of early infant regulation
and later behavior in play interviews. Child
Development 30:211–216.
Fannin, Leon F., and Marshall B. Clinard
1965   Differences in the conception of self as a

male among lower and middle class delin-
quents. Social Problems 13:205–214.

Farberow, Norman L., and Edwin S. Shneidman, eds.
1961   The cry for help. New York, McGraw-Hill.

Ferenczi, Sandor
1914   The nosology of male homosexuality. *In*
Sex in psychoanalysis. Ernest Jones, trans.
New York, Basic Books, 1950.

Ferraro, Thomas, and R. Jay Turner
n.d.   Division of labor within the family. Mimeographed.

Forbes, Gilbert B.
1964   Lean body mass and fat in obese children.
Pediatrics 34:308–314.
1965   Toward a new dimension in human growth.
Borden award address, October, 1964.
Pediatrics 36:825–835.

Franck, Kate
n.d.   Franck Drawing Completion Test: preliminary manual. Melbourne, Australia, Aus-
tralian Council for Educational Research.

Franck, Kate, and E. Rosen
1949   A projective test of masculinity-femininity.
Journal of Consulting Psychology 13:247–
256.

Freud, Sigmund
1923   The ego and the id. Standard Edition, 19:12–
66. London, Hogarth Press, 1961.

Gerall, Arnold A.
1966   Hormonal factors influencing masculine behavior of female guinea pigs. Journal of
Comparative and Physiological Psychology
62:365–369.

Gonen, Yechiel, and Leonard M. Lansky
1965   Masculinity, femininity, and masculinity-
femininity: a phenomenological study of the
Mf scale of the MMPI. Paper read at the 36th
Annual Meeting of the Eastern Psychological Association, Atlantic City, N. J.

Goodenough, Evelyn W.
    1957   Interest in persons as an aspect of sex dif-
           ferences in the early years. Genetic Psychol-
           ogy Monographs 55:287–323.
Gough, Harrison G.
    1952   Identifying psychological femininity. Edu-
           cational and Psychological Measurement
           12:427–439.
Green, Elise H.
    1933   Friendships and quarrels among preschool
           children. Child Development 4:236–252.
Greenstein, Jules M.
    1966   Father characteristics and sex typing. Journal
           of Personality and Social Psychology 3:271–
           277.
Hamburg, David A. and Donald T. Lunde
    1966   Sex hormones in the development of sex
           differences in human behavior. In The devel-
           opment of sex differences, E. E. Maccoby,
           ed. Stanford, Calif., Stanford University
           Press.
Harman, Harry H.
    1960   Modern factor analysis. Chicago, University
           of Chicago Press.
Harrington, Charles
    n.d.   Anthropology of conflict and aggression. Un-
           published manuscript.
    1968   Sexual differentiation in socialization and
           some male genital mutilations. American
           Anthropologist 70:952–956.
Harrington, Charles, and Mary Lou Wilkins
    1966   Treating the social symptoms of mental
           illness. Hospital and Community Psychiatry
           17:136–138.
Hartley, R. E.
    1960   Children's concepts of male and female
           roles. Merrill-Palmer Quarterly 6:83–91.
Hartup, W. W., and Y. Himino
    1959   Social isolation vs. interaction with adults

in relation to aggression in preschool children. Journal of Abnormal and Social Psychology 59:17–22.

Hattwick, Laberta
1937 Sex differences in the behavior of nursery school children. Child Development 8:343–355.

Herzberg, F., and M. Lepkin
1954 A study of sex differences on the Primary Mental Abilities Test. Educational Psychological Measurement 17:687–689.

Hetherington, E. M.
1965 A developmental study of the effects of sex of the dominant parent on sex-role preference, identification, and imitation in children. Journal of Personality and Social Psychology 2:188–194.

Hettinger, T.
1961 Physiology of strength. Springfield, Ill., Charles C Thomas, Publisher.

Hollingshead, August B.
1952 Two factor index of social position. Mimeographed.

Hooker, Evelyn
1965 An empirical study of some relations between sexual pattern and gender identity in male homosexuals. In Sex research, John Money, ed. New York, Holt, Rinehart, & Winston.

Housden, J.
1965 An examination of the biologic etiology of transvestism. International Journal of Social Psychiatry 11:301–305.

Howe, James
1966 Caymanian drinking behavior. Honors thesis, Department of Anthropology, Harvard University.

Jersild, A. T., and F. V. Markey
1935 Conflicts between preschool children. Child Development Monographs 21.

Johnson, M.
   1963   Sex-role learning in the nuclear family.
          Child Development 34:319–333.
Kagan, Jerome
   1964   Acquisition and significance of sex typing
          and sex-role identity. *In* Review of child
          development research, M. L. Hoffman and L.
          Hoffman, eds. New York, Russell Sage Foun-
          dation.
Kagan, Jerome, and Howard A. Moss
   1962   Birth to maturity: a study in psychological
          development. New York, Wiley.
Katz, Phyllis
   1959   Responses of young children to the Franck
          Test. Unpublished term paper, Yale Uni-
          versity, reported in Kohlberg, 1966.
Kinsey, A. C., W. B. Pomeroy, and C. E. Martin
   1948   Sexual behavior in the human male. Phila-
          delphia, W. B. Saunders.
Kohlberg, Lawrence
   1966   A cognitive-developmental analysis of chil-
          dren's sex-role concepts and attitudes. *In*
          The development of sex differences, E. E.
          Maccoby, ed. Stanford, Calif., Stanford Uni-
          versity Press.
Kohn, M. L.
   1959   Social class and parental values. American
          Journal of Sociology 64:337–351.
Kostick, M. M.
   1954   A study of transfer: sex differences in the
          reasoning process. Journal of Educational
          Psychology 45:449–458.
Lacey, J. I. and B. C. Lacey
   1958   The relationship of resting autonomic activ-
          ity to motor impulsivity. Research Publica-
          tions of the Association of Nervous and Mental
          Diseases 36:144–209.
Lansky, Leonard M.
   1964   The family structure also affects the model:

sex-role identification in parents of preschool children. Merrill-Palmer Quarterly 10:39–50.

1965   References to the Franck Drawing Completion Test. Mimeographed.

Lansky, Leonard M., Vaughn J. Crandell, Jerome Kagan, and Charles T. Baker
1961   Sex differences in aggression and its correlates in middle-class adolescents. Child Development 32:45–58.

Lewis, Oscar
1951   Life in a Mexican village. Urbana, University of Illinois Press.

Linton, Ralph
1936   The study of man. New York, Appleton-Century-Crofts.

Lipsitt, P. D. and F. L. Strodtbeck
1967   Defensiveness in decision making as a function of sex-role identification. Journal of Personality and Social Psychology 6:10–15.

Levine, Seymour
1966   Sex differences in the brain. Scientific American 214:84–90.

Lopata, Helena Z.
1965   The secondary features of primary relationships. Human Organization 24:116–123.

Lynn, D. B., and W. L. Sawrey
1958   The effects of father absence on Norwegian boys and girls. Journal of Abnormal and Social Psychology 55:76–87.

Maccoby, Eleanor E.
1959   Role taking in childhood and its consequences for social learning. Child Development 30:239–252.

McCandless, B. R., C. B. Bilous, and H. L. Bennett
1961   Peer popularity and dependence on adults in preschool age socialization. Child Development 32:511–518.

McElroy, W. A.
1954 A sex difference in preference for shapes. British Journal of Psychology 45:209–216.
McKee, J. P., and F. B. Leader
1955 The relationship of socioeconomic status and aggression to the competitive behavior of preschool children. Child Development 26:135–142.
McNemar, Quinn
1962 Psychological statistics. New York, Wiley.
Mead, Margaret
1935 Sex and temperament, New York, Morrow.
Meadows, A. W.
1959 Review of Franck Drawing Completion Test. *In* The fifth mental measurements yearbook, O. K. Buros, ed. Highland Park, N. J. Gryphon Press. 234.
Miller, Walter
1958 Lower class culture as a generating milieu of gang delinquency. *In* The sociology of crime and delinquency, M. E. Wolfgang, L. Savitz, and N. Johnson, eds. New York, Wiley.
1964 The corner gang boys get married. Family Life Coordinator 13:47–48. Reprinted from Transaction 1:10–12.
Milton, G. A.
1957 The effects of sex-role identification upon problem solving skill. Journal of Abnormal and Social Psychology 55:208–212.
Minturn, Leigh, and William W. Lambert
1964 Mothers of six cultures. New York, Wiley.
Money, John
1965 Psychosexual differentiation. *In* Sex research; new developments, J. Money, ed. New York, Holt, Rinehart & Winston.
Moore, T., and L. E. Ucko
1961 Four to six: constructiveness and conflict in

meeting doll play problems. Journal of Child Psychology and Psychiatry 2:21–47.

Munroe, Robert L.
n.d. A cross cultural study of the couvade. Unpublished manuscript.
1964 Couvade practices among the Black Carib. Unpublished Ph.D. thesis. Harvard University.

Munroe, Robert L., Ruth H. Munroe, and John W. M. Whiting
1965 Structure and sentiment: evidence from recent studies of the couvade. Paper read at American Anthropological Association meeting, Denver, Colo.

Murdock, George
1936 Comparative data on the division of labor by sex. Social Forces 15:551–553.

Mussen, P., and L. Distler
1959 Masculinity, identification, and father-son relationship. Journal of Abnormal and Social Psychology 59:350–356.

Muste, Myra J., and D. F. Sharpe
1947 Some influential factors in the determination of aggressive behavior in preschool children. Child Development 18:11–28.

Needham, Rodney
1962 Structure and sentiment. Chicago, University of Chicago Press.

Osgood, Charles E., George J. Suci, and Percy H. Tannenbaum
1957 The measurement of meaning. Urbana, University of Illinois Press.

Parsons, Talcott, and R. F. Bales
1955 The family and socialization. New York, Free Press.

Piaget, Jean
1962 Play, dreams and imitation in childhood. New York, Norton.

Rabban, M.
1950 Sex-role identification in young children in two diverse social groups. Genetic Psychology Monographs 42:81–158.

Robins, Lee N.
1966 Deviant children grown up. Baltimore, Williams & Wilkins.

Rohrer, John H., and Munro Edmonson
1960 The eighth generation. New York, Harper & Row.

Rosenberg, B. G., and B. Sutton-Smith
1964 Ordinal position and sex-role identification. Genetic Psychology Monographs 70: 297–328.

Scheff, Thomas
1966 Being mentally ill. Chicago, Aldine.

Sears, Robert R.
1965 Development of gender role. *In* Sex and behavior, Frank A. Beach, ed. New York, Wiley.

Sears, Robert R., Eleanor E. Maccoby, and Harry Levin
1957 Patterns of child rearing. Evanston, Ill. Row, Peterson.

Sears, Robert R., M. H. Pintler, and P. S. Sears
1946 Effect of father separation on preschool children's doll play aggression. Child development 17:219–243.

Sears, Robert R., Lucy Rau, and Richard Alpert
1966 Identification and child rearing. London, Tavistock.

Sears, Robert R., John W. M. Whiting, V. Nowlis, and P. S. Sears
1953 Some child rearing antecedents of aggression and dependency in young children. Genetic Psychology Monographs 47:135–234.

Sheldon, W. H.
1949 Varieties of delinquent youth. New York, Harper & Row.

Strong, E. K.
  1943   Vocational interests of men and women.
         Stanford, Calif., Stanford University Press.
Suttles, Gerald S.
  1968   The social order of the slum. Chicago, Uni-
         versity of Chicago Press.
Terman, L. M., and C. C. Miles
  1936   Sex and personality. New York, Macmillan.
Udry, J. Richard
  1966   Marital instability by race, sex, education,
         and occupation using 1960 census data. Amer-
         ican Journal of Sociology 72:203–209.
Vener, Arthur M., and Clinton A. Snyder
  1966   The preschool child's awareness and antici-
         pation of adult sex-roles. Sociometry 29:159–
         168.
Vroegh, Karen, and Milicent Handridge
  1966   Sex-role typing in the preschool years: an
         overview. Research Program in Child Devel-
         opment, Chicago, Ill. Institute for Juvenile
         Research Publications, Research Reports,
         vol. 3, no. 13.
Walters, J., Doris Pearce, and Lucille Dahms
  1957   Affectional and aggressive behavior of pre-
         school children. Child Development 28:15–
         26.
Webb, A. P.
  1963   Sex-role preference and adjustment in early
         adolescents. Child Development 34:609–618.
White, Robert W.
  1963   Ego and reality in psychoanalytic theory.
         Psychological Issues 3:Monograph 11.
Whiting, Beatrice
  1963   Six cultures: studies of child rearing. New
         York, Wiley.
  1965   Sex identity conflict and physical violence:
         a comparative study. American Anthropolo-
         gist 67:123–140.

Whiting, John W. M.
   1960   Resource mediation and learning by identi-
           fication. *In* Personality development in chil-
           dren, I. Iscoe and H. Stevenson, eds. Austin,
           University of Texas Press.
   1962   Comment. American Journal of Sociology
           67:391–393.
Whiting, John W. M., Richard Kluckhohn, and Albert
   Anthony
   1958   The function of male initiation ceremonies
           at puberty. *In* Readings in social psychology,
           3rd ed., Eleanor E. Maccoby, Theodore M.
           Newcomb, and Eugene L. Hartley, eds.
           New York, Holt, Rinehart & Winston. 359–
           370.
Wolanski, Napoleon
   1967   Basic problems in physical development in
           man in relation to the evaluation of develop-
           ment of children and youth. Current Anthro-
           pology 8:35–60.
Young, Frank
   1962   The function of male initiation ceremonies:
           a cross-cultural test of an alternative hypothe-
           sis. American Journal of Sociology 67:379–
           391.
   1965   Initiation ceremonies: a cross-cultural study
           of status dramatization. New York, Bobbs-
           Merrill.